DYNAMIC CUSTOMIZATION

DYNAMIC CUSTOMIZATION

Release Type, Axis Stability, and Optimum Pin Carry

Robert Strickland

Robert H. Strickland Associates, Everett, WA 98206-1388

Cover and book design: Robert H. Strickland, Sue Strickland

Cover photo: Jankaliciak, Creative Graphic Arts, York, North Yorkshire, UK; via Dreamstime LLC, Brentwood, TN 37027

Typesetting: Robert H. Strickland

ISBN 10: 0963591924 / ISBN 13: 9780963591920

Library of Congress Control Number: 2011914527

Copyright 2011 by Robert Strickland

All rights reserved. No part of this book may be reproduced or transmitted in any form or by any means, electronic or mechanical, including photocopying, recording or by any information storage or retrieval system, without permission in writing from the publisher

First Printing 2011

Printed in the United States of America

Robert H. Strickland Associates
P O Box 1388, Everett, WA 98206-1388

Contents

	Preface	9
	Disclaimer	11
	Acknowledgements	13
1	**Dynamic Customization**	15
	Why Dynamically-imbalanced Balls?	16
	Why Dynamically-balanced Balls?	17
	The Challenge	18
2	**What You Need to Know**	19
	Static Dodo Scale	19
	Types of Release	19
	Ball Design and Construction	20
	Ball Dynamics	21
3	**Release Type**	23
	Determining Release Type	25
	Using Release Type Information	26
4	**Ball Design and Construction**	29
	Two-piece Construction	29
	Three-piece Construction	31
	Modern Design Considerations	32
	Accidentally Shifted Core	32
	Deliberately Offset Core	33
	Asymmetric Core	34
	Factors Influencing Ball Choice	35

    Ball to Lane Friction 35
    Total Ball Weight 35
    Weight Centers 36
    Handedness 37
    Hand Position 37

5 Bowling Ball Dynamics 39
    Weight Centers 39
    Moment of Inertia 40
    Gyroscopic Motion 42
    Precession 43
        Torque-free Precession 43
        Torque-induced Precession 43
    Positive Axis Weight vs. Negative Axis Weight 46
    Stability vs. Instability 48
        Effective Mass 49
        Lope 50
        Wobble 51
    Modern Layouts 52

6 Recommendations for Various Release Types 55
    Goal 55
    Organization 56
    Full Roller 59
        Ball Selection 60
        Layout 61
        Post-drilling Adjustments 61
    Importance of Adhering to the S-P Line 62
    High Roller 63
        Ball Selection 64
        Layout 65
        Post-drilling Adjustments 65
    Low Roller 66
        Ball Selection 67
        Layout 69
        Post-drilling Adjustments 69

High Spinner 70
Ball Selection 71
Layout 72
Post-drilling Adjustments 72
Low Spinner 73
Ball Selection 74
Layout 75
Post-drilling Adjustments 75

7 Layout and Adjustment 77
Procedure for a Two-piece Ball 77
Preparation of the New Ball Before Drilling 78
Finding the Track on a Previously-drilled Ball 78
Laying Out the New Ball 80
Post-Drilling Adjustments 82
Procedure for a Three-piece Ball 84
Thoughts About the Location of an Extra Hole 86
Into an Axis Pole 86
Into the Resultant Static Center 87
Into the Pin 87
Anywhere Else 87
Tips for Observing Pin Carry 88
Test Lane Condition 88
Settling Down 88
Keeping Track 89
Interpretation 89
Action 90

Index 97
Figures 103
Tables 105

Preface

I began fitting and drilling bowling balls in 1964 in Jim Hensley's Pro Shop at Zangs Bowl in Dallas, Texas. Since then, I have drilled all of my own equipment and that of many others. By the time I began writing articles about bowling ball dynamics for the **International Bowlers Journal's Pro Shop Forum**, in the 1980s, I had been a keen student of the bowling delivery, equipment, and scoring environment for several years (thanks mainly to Bill Taylor) and had written **Perceptive Bowling**.

By that time, the two-piece bowling ball had joined the three-piece ball on the market. The two-piece ball had an outwardly-visible factory pin in addition to the customary punch mark that indicated, at least on the surface, the ball's center of gravity. Now, there were two weight centers to deal with, and shop professionals placed these in a myriad of positions while experimenting on their customers. As I discovered later, many of these layouts caused problems with pocket pin carry or their tracks ran over the grip holes.

In an attempt to gain a piece of the bowling ball market, one manufacturer supplied a sheet of suggested grip layouts with each ball. It was entitled, **Twenty Six Ways to Drill the XXX Ball** (XXX = the manufacturer's name; omitted for obvious reasons!). It was not long before I began to refer to this document as **Twenty Six Ways to Ruin a Ball**.

I selected one layout that suggested I place the factory pin above the fingerholes and the punch mark (static center) somewhere near the center of the grip. This particular layout seemed reasonable because it placed the factory pin and associated weight center close to where the rotating force was to be imparted by the fingers.

I drilled and finished the new ball and quickly took it to the (blocked and quite high-scoring) lanes for an enthusiastic trial. After a few warm-up frames, *I scored one practice game with ten solid pocket hits. I bowled one strike, one 8-10 split, two 4-9 splits, two 4-pin leaves, one 8-pin leave, and three 10-pin leaves.*

Disgusted, I immediately took the ball back into the shop and plugged it completely. While I waited for the plug to cure, I sat down and tried to figure out what had happened! I finally worked out a layout style that would stabilize the axis of rotation. I drilled this new layout and practiced with the ball. It was a superior-carrying ball, and I used it for a long time, until it was misappropriated during a teaching tour of Europe.

While teaching bowling form and pro shop skills over the next few years, I added to and refined this successful layout into a system that could benefit bowlers of various release types. I call this system **Dynamic Customization**, and, *rather than fitting internal imbalances to particular oil dressing patterns, it fits internal imbalances to release type*. I lectured about this method but never offered complete instructions in a printed form.

Although manufacturers include drilling guides with new balls, many of their layouts are similar to each other and do not take into account the various release types. They are designed mainly to lengthen skid and delay the break point, giving the ball an acute angle of attack to the pocket. That being said, the friction between reactive resin balls and blocked, synthetic lane surfaces, along with low pin resistance are mainly responsible for today's wildly high-scoring bowling environment; the layouts are less significant.

As important as fitting a proper grip, **Dynamic Customization** is easy to master and minimizes confusion, allowing bowlers to turn their attention toward refining their forms, sharpening their ability to hit targets, and building confidence.

The text is generously bolded to facilitate skimming. Explanations of ball dynamics in this book are as simple as possible, so the reader may apply the principles without having to ponder a myriad of symbols, equations, and data. I hope that you use the information to help yourself and others for whom you provide services. See the **Disclaimer**, below.

Bob Strickland, 2011
bob@roberthstrickland.com

Disclaimer

The layouts described in this book, like those recommended by others, may not be effective for all persons. Some factors that may cause a failure to satisfy include improper ball selection, lack of care in fitting the grip, unauthorized modification of a layout, inadequate observation, and improper location of an extra hole, to name a few. *Therefore, the author/publisher disclaims any responsibility and liability in connection with any actions taken or not taken based on the content of this book.*

Acknowledgements

Thanks to my wonderful wife, Sue, a lifelong bowler, who has learned the sport thoroughly and has taught right along with me from the start. I would not have had the great adventures and successes without her guidance, support, and love.

Special thanks to Dr. Ron Huston, Professor Emeritus of Mechanics and Distinguished Research Professor in the Mechanical Engineering Department at the University of Cincinnati, for his critical review of this book and helpful suggestions.

After Bill Taylor challenged the bowling world to think of bowling balls as gyroscopes, he introduced me to Dr. Huston. It was during a brief conversation with Dr. Huston in 1981 that I began to devise the layout system that is the subject of this book.

Sincere thanks to the following persons in whose pro shops I developed skills that continue to help myself and others:

- Al Flores, Wilmington, California
- Bob Stiles, Houston, Texas
- Bob Tomlinson and Roy "Pete" Moore, Dallas Texas
- Earl Pichette and Clint Hunter, Dallas, Texas
- Jim Hensley, Austin, Texas
- John Vavala, Jr., Wilmington, Delaware
- Ken Cousson, Athens, Georgia
- Kirk Kinnamon, Portland, Oregon
- Rex Blair, Dallas Texas

Perpetual thanks go to the following persons whose keen minds, experience, and love of the sport allowed them to share valuable information about the bowling environment:

Bill Lillard, Houston, Texas
Bill Taylor, San Gabriel, California
Bob Chase, Kansas City, Kansas
Buddy Bomar, Chicago, Illinois
Carmen Salvino, Chicago, Illinois
Cecil Caddel, Mesquite, Texas
David Brewster, Carrollton, Texas
J. B. Solomon, Dallas, Texas
J. D. Amburgey, Odessa, Texas
Bob Blakeslee, Bellingham, Washington
Christopher Olfson, Antioch, California
Jim and Cina Goodwin, Rockwall, Texas
Jim Lampson, St. Louis, Missouri
Joe Norris, San Diego, California
Johnny Cerminaro, Dallas, Texas
Jon Jensen, Mount Vernon, Washington
Keith Little, Dallas, Texas
Kurt Gengelbach, Carrollton, Texas
Tom Kelly, Omaha, Nebraska
Tony Lindemann, Dallas, Texas
Vincent "Viny" Yetitto, Port Chester, New York
W. J. "Red" Childers, Dallas, Texas

Thanks to dedicated shop professionals, many of whom attended my workshops, that keep up a daily struggle to make a positive impact on their customers.

Special thanks go to my Cairn Terriers, Mac, Bobby, and Dougal, who have always waited patiently by my side during my writing projects.

1 Dynamic Customization

Picture a ball delivered two times with good form, impacting squarely into the pocket, one yielding a strong 9-pin leave, while the other yielding a weak 10-pin leave. Both shots appear to have been made similarly enough for identical pocket hits to yield identical results, but because the weight centers were not placed appropriately, the ball took two different paths through the rack of pins. *Such undesirable outcomes can be minimized.*

Dynamic Customization is a method of placing an imbalance (all weight centers combined, as described herein) within a bowling ball to favor consistency in the way the ball (1) rolls down the lane (***dynamics***) and (2) proceeds through the rack of pins with optimal ***deflection***. It is a ball selection and layout style that takes into account an individual bowler's type of release, as indicated by the track on the surface of the ball. Five basic release types are shown in Figure 1.

Figure 1: Five Basic Release Types

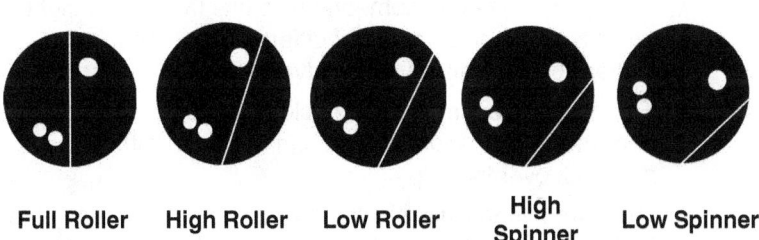

Full Roller   **High Roller**   **Low Roller**   **High Spinner**   **Low Spinner**

The following discussion relates to these definitions:
- **Imbalance** – the collective **mass** of all weight centers within the ball. **Imbalanced** means a lack of stability, the ball's internal weight centers, or masses, are not in symmetry around the ball's axis of rotation.
- **Deflection** – a change in direction of the ball resulting from an off-center impact with a pin.
- **Dynamics** – the behavior of a ball in translational (straight) and gyroscopic (rotating) motion on the lane.

Why Dynamically-imbalanced Balls?

Because of the friction between **reactive resin** balls and **blocked** synthetic lanes and the elasticity of modern bowling pins, new balls can be spectacularly high-scoring or low-scoring, depending on the state of the lane condition and the experience of the player using them. Quite naturally, high scores draw everyone's attention.

High-interest, recreational bowlers want to compete on a level with skilled players. In hopes of improving, they try imbalanced balls with layouts that they see being drilled in pro shops Basically, they seek a shortcut to success.

It cannot be denied that some of the manufacturers' suggested layouts, when properly applied by experienced shop professionals, give acceptable results leading to improved scores. **However, the majority of grip layouts recommended by manufacturers have the following shortcomings**:

- They are targeted to someone who hits the pocket eight times a game on a variety of different lane conditions. Better bowlers still have the advantage.
- Factory pin placements are in close proximity to the fingerholes so that all bowlers can use them without running the track over the grip holes.
- Most are dynamically similar to each other in delaying the ball's break point to create an acute angle of attack to the pocket that can present problems of control.
- Not necessarily relating to the bowler's release type, they often result in unpredictable leaves from pocket hits and difficult, multiple-pin combinations when the pocket is missed.

Why Dynamically-balanced Balls?

The goal of serious recreational bowlers should be consistency of roll and optimal deflection, leading to enhanced pin carry. *Dynamic Customization* attempts to accomplish this goal.

The method of achieving *Dynamic Customization* is different from most of the drilling instructions included with new bowling balls. *Its purpose is to maximize pin carry on solid pocket hits for an individual's release type without regard to making the ball's visible reaction take on any particular shape.*

Like all other layouts, *Dynamic Customization* involves manipulation of the skid, roll, and hook characteristics of the ball, using surface properties, total ball weight, and internal weight distribution to effect change. However, *Dynamic Customization begins with a potentially-stabilized, loaded axis and adjusts the position of the break point and the pattern of deflection to optimize pin carry on pocket hits.*

Occasionally, manufacturers include a layout somewhat similar to those described herein, but there is usually no emphasis on a particular release type except the full roller. The basic differences between the goals of manufacturers and those of *Dynamic Customization* are presented in Table 1. The terms used in descriptions are defined in subsequent chapters; see *Glossary*.

Table 1: Differences Between Goals

Characteristic	Manufacturers' Goal	Dynamic Customization Goal
Skid	Lengthen skid through ball surface selection and destabilize axis to delay break point.	Adjust skid through selection of ball surface; lengthen skid slightly through early imbalance; no emphasis placed on position of break point.
Roll	No emphasis placed on length of roll phase.	Length of roll phase long enough to allow axis to stabilize.

Table 1:   Differences Between Goals

Characteristic	Manufacturers' Goal	Dynamic Customization Goal
Hook	Sharply breaking hook; begins from delayed break point with additional flip reaction to augment angle of attack.	No particular shape to hook; no significant delay of break point; no flip reaction as axis is stabilized in advance of or close to break point.
Lope / Wobble	Emphasis placed on destabilized axis to accomplish steeper angle of attack.	Stabilize axis, eliminating lope and wobble as soon as possible to take advantage of precession.
Deflection Pattern	No emphasis; possibly through selection of appropriate total ball weight.	In harmony with total ball weight, optimize deflection pattern to maximize pin carry.
Pin Carry	Widen pocket through steep angle of attack, no emphasis on accuracy or unusual leaves.	Increase frequency of pin carry on solid pocket hits.

The Challenge

A major concern, at this writing, is that balls are being drilled with little or no attention paid to the way bowlers release them. Significant numbers of bowlers are therefore provided with dynamically unstable balls that show somewhat useful skid, roll, hook patterns only because of today's ubiquitous blocked lane conditions. Their equipment could be chosen and laid out to be more useful on a variety of conditions.

Release type involves hand position, forward swing speed, angle of the ball to the lane surface, and the force of rotation at release. A release type depends on the physical limitations of the bowler. Just like the bowler employing it, a release type has its own strengths and weaknesses, as described in **Recommendations for Various Release Types**; the challenge is to compensate for these weaknesses through use of an appropriate layout.

2 What You Need to Know

Before you can **Dynamically Customize** a ball, you must have knowledge and skill in the following areas:

Static Dodo Scale

Be able to use a static balance (dodo scale) to determine the amount and location of a static imbalance within a ball.

Total ball weight and static (unmoving) imbalances are measured and located on a dodo scale. In the industry-accepted technique, the ball is weighed motionless on three planes — top/bottom, finger/thumb, and right/left lateral, with the reference point being the **static center** in an undrilled ball and the **grip center** in a drilled ball. Dynamic imbalances cannot be measured on this device.

If you need to learn how to weigh a ball on this device, read Bill Taylor's booklet, **Weighing a Bowling Ball for Balance and Imbalance**. Practice by weighing new, undrilled balls for which the total weight and top weight are indicated on the factory box.

Types of Release

Understand essential differences among five types of release, as shown by the diameter and location of the track on the ball.

There are five release types — Full, High, and Low Roller, and High and Low Spinner — and knowledge of a type gives insight into its pattern of skid, roll, and hook, its tendency to carry pins, and into the useful placement of internal imbalances in the ball relative to the grip. These topics are discussed thoroughly in **Release Type** and **Recommendations for Various Release Types**.

Ball Design and Construction

Understand the major differences in construction (shell, core, weight centers) among the various ball brands and models.

Modern bowling balls are marketed with different types of construction, based on the relative densities of the shell and core. Balls that used be called **shell-dense** (*cover-dense*) are now referred to as **high RG**, RG standing for **radius of gyration**. Others that used to be called **core-dense** are now referred to as **low RG**. See **Ball Design and Construction**.

Some factors depend on ball selection:

- **Size of hook.** Desired size of hook should be selected on the basis of ball surface characteristics.
- **Deflection.** The pattern of deflection through the rack of pins can be adjusted by total ball weight and positioning of weight centers relative to the ball's axis of rotation. *The lighter the total weight of the ball, the wider the path taken through the pins.*
- **Track diameter.** The diameter of a bowler's track relates to pin carry and deflection and tends to remain the same from one high RG ball to another. However, *a low RG ball tends to roll more circumferentially, increasing the diameter of a bowler's track*. Track diameter can also be adjusted by the positioning of weight centers relative to the ball's axis of rotation.
- **Ball dynamics.** Position of the break point and angle of attack can be adjusted appropriately for release type, ball speed, and handedness. See **Bowling Ball Dynamics**.

The location of an imbalance relative to the axis can have an effect on the dynamic characteristics typically associated with a particular ball's design. Depending on where the imbalance is placed, a high RG ball may act more like a low RG ball and vice versa. See **Positive Axis Weight vs. Negative Axis Weight**.

Ball Dynamics

Understand how the weight and location of internal weight centers influence the way a ball acts when it is rolling down the lane and when it hits the pins.

When not in contact with a surface, like a spinning golf ball in flight, or when in contact with a surface, like a bowling ball rolling down a lane, the ball is in **gyroscopic motion**. The ball's mass moves in a circle around its **axis of rotation,** or more simply, its **axis**, an imaginary line perpendicular to the plane of rotation and passing through the center of the ball.

As shown in Figure 2, the axis is perpendicular to the plane of the ball track; equidistant from all points on the track (the track is **radially** equidistant from the axis), passing through the geometric center of the ball. The axis has a **positive axis pole** (**PAP**) at one end; oriented toward the center of the lane, and a **negative axis pole** at the other end, oriented toward the bowler's **swingside** channel.

Figure 2: The Ball's Axis of Rotation

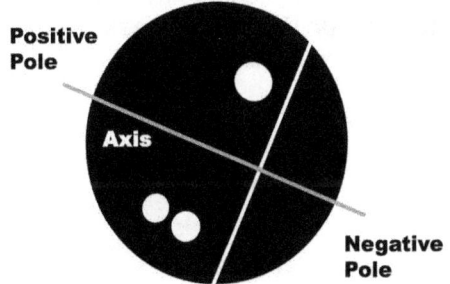

It is possible to place a weight center on the axis of rotation to stabilize a rolling ball or off of the axis of rotation to destabilize it. A weight center of a given magnitude has a greater effect on a lighter weight ball. For example, a weight center of 2.5 ounces has a greater potential of influencing the dynamics of a 14-pound ball than those of a 15-pound ball. Therefore, weight center positioning must be carefully planned. See **Bowling Ball Dynamics**.

The track flares if the imbalance is not on the axis of rotation.
This flare is visible evidence of wobble (axis gyration) and the generation of skid through destabilizing the axis of rotation of the ball.

Figure 3: Flare of the Track

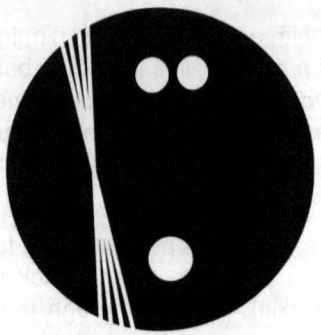

Note: Early axis gyration is beneficial to help the ball through the head of the lane, but the axis should stabilize before ball impact with the pins. The suggested layouts in the chapter titled ***Recommendations for Various Release Types*** stabilize the ball for some distance before it hits the pins.

---

3 Release Type

A release type is characterized by the position and action of the hand during the release of the ball. During the forward swing, the fingers and the thumb hold the ball in an orientation relative to (1) the intended trajectory (for example, **staying behind** or **being on the side** of the ball) and (2) the lane surface (the ball's axis pointed downward, parallel with, or pointed upward).

After the exit of the thumb, the fingers lift the ball onto the lane surface, imparting rotation. The angle of this rotation to the lane surface depends on the orientation of the hand. This orientation, along with any rotation of the wrist, establishes the angle of the ball's axis of rotation to the swing plane and lane surface and accounts for the diameter and position of the track on the ball. Figure 4 shows the influence of the hand position along the swing plane on the angle of the axis to the lane.

Figure 4: Swing Plane Hand Position vs. Axis Angle

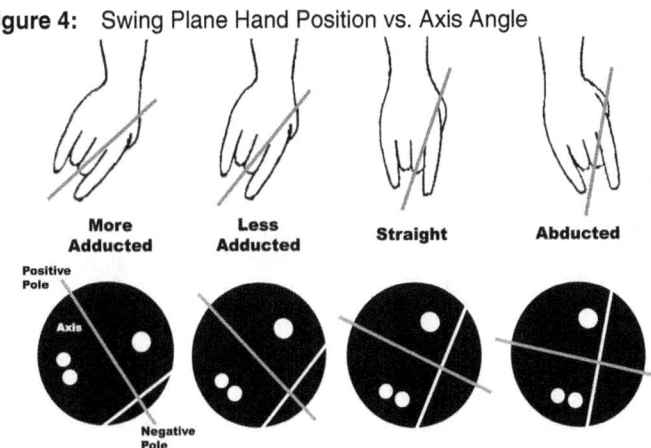

The spherical diameter and location of the track are used to classify release types. Because there is a continuum of release types — one type overlaps another — it is convenient to use five categories described by Bill Taylor in his book, **Balance**, in discussion The spherical diameter and location of the track are used to classify release types. Table 2 summarizes these types and describes the actions causing them. *The illustrations of balls and tracks in this book are diagrammatic and are not intended to be accurate depictions.*

Table 2: Release Types and Causative Actions

Release Type	Action	Explanation
Full Roller		The hand position in line with the forward swing begins with a straight wrist and the hand on the side of the ball. Just before the thumb exits, the hand adducts at the wrist and rotates from inside to outside. The thumb drags on exit, adjusting the axis angle to vertical.
High Roller		The hand position in line with the forward swing is rather straight, and this orientation is maintained throughout the release. The hand is typically slightly behind the ball to give a little turn of the wrist during the release.
Low Roller		The hand position in line with the forward swing shows slight adduction of the wrist throughout the release. The hand is typically behind the ball to give a little more turn of the wrist during the release than the high roller.

Table 2: Release Types and Causative Actions

Release Type	Action	Explanation
High Spinner		The hand position in line with the forward swing shows moderate adduction of the wrist during the forward swing and throughout the release. The hand is quite far behind the ball to give a moderate turn of the wrist during the release.
Low Spinner		The hand position in line with the forward swing shows maximum adduction of the wrist during the forward swing and throughout the release. The hand is typically very far behind the ball to give a maximum turn of the wrist.

Determining Release Type

Follow these steps to classify a release type from the track on a currently-used, *properly-fitted* ball.

1. Trace over the track with wax pencil to make it easier to see. If one is available, use a ball with a narrow track. If the track shows an obvious flare, trace as closely as possible to the center.

2. Measure the track's **spherical diameter** (SD). The spherical diameter is the distance measured in an arc over the center of the smallest portion of the ball enclosed by the track, as shown in Figure 5. A *high track* is one with a large spherical diameter, while a *low track* is one with a small spherical diameter.

Figure 5: Spherical Diameter of a Track on a Ball

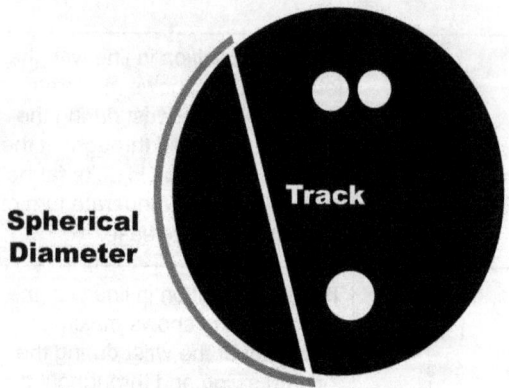

The smaller the spherical diameter, the greater the tilt of the axis of rotation when the ball is rolling down the lane.

3. Measure the angle of the track to the grip layout centerline.
4. Compare the track's spherical diameter to those listed in the tables in *Recommendations for Various Release Types*. The information given for a track with a spherical diameter closest to that of the currently-used ball applies.

Using Release Type Information

The overall sequence of procedures for *Dynamic Customization* from start to finish is summarized briefly below.

1. Determine the release type from the track on a currently-used ball, using the procedure described above.
2. Select a new symmetric-core ball based on its design, whether two-piece or three-piece, following the applicable suggestions under *Recommendations for Various Release Types*.
3. Lay out the new ball, following the applicable sequence of steps described in *Layout and Adjustment*.

   The important adjustment phase must be given adequate time, because it involves serious observation of pin-carrying behavior of the new ball and may require the drilling of an additional hole.

4. Follow-up involves additional observation of ball behavior and occasionally may require adding plug material back into the extra hole in the axis poles. See *"Tips for Observing Pin Carry" in Layout and Adjustment.*

4 Ball Design and Construction

The way a ball is constructed determines how far a ball may skid, when it may assume a roll, and the angle of attack to the pocket. Determining factors include the friction potential of the shell material, the relative density between shell and core, and the number, magnitude, and location of any weight centers inside the ball.

As recent as the late 1980s, there were basically only two types of ball: three-piece and two-piece. A bit of historical information about older brands of ball is helpful to understanding differences in design. Because current ball designs are more complicated and come and go on the market more often than in years past, no specific brand of modern ball is discussed.

Two-piece Construction

A two-piece ball consists of a core and a shell, shown in Figure 6. The core of two-piece balls is denser than the shell. To achieve top weight, the core is more oblong from top to bottom. Alternatively, it can be given a lobe that sticks out from the core. The resulting weight center is denser than the shell, providing the top weight necessary to compensate for material removed when the grip holes are drilled or to shift for dynamic effect. If a symmetric core remains exactly in the center of the mold when the shell is poured, the shell is of uniform thickness around the core's axis, and the ball's static center lies in the center of the factory pin.

Figure 6: Construction of a Two-piece Ball

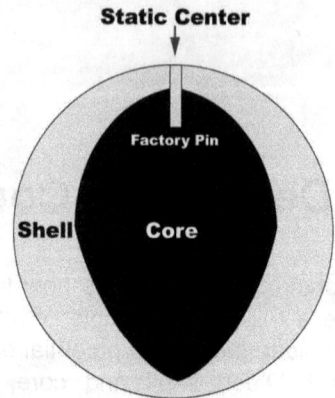

The two-piece category included FAB's Hammer, Roto-Grip's Grenade, and AMF's Cobra balls. All of these had dense cores and deeply-placed weight centers. Today, these would all be classified as low RG.

Because the centers of gravity of two-piece balls are usually closer to the geometric center of the ball, they tend to offer less resistance to the force of lift, but they typically skid less and roll sooner. Therefore, a two-piece, low RG ball can benefit a bowler whose normal release type makes his ball skid a longer distance and roll later. Examples of release types that can benefit from a low RG are the full roller and low spinner.

Some two-piece balls have a high RG. These are more versatile for the shop professional because their shallow weight centers have larger moments of inertia and can exert a greater influence on the dynamics of the ball. An imbalance can be placed further away from the positive axis pole to maximize skid and minimize roll. Or, it can be placed closer to the positive axis pole to both enhance skid and maximize roll. Equally important, the imbalance can be positioned toward the negative axis pole to lessen skid and induce even earlier roll. The dynamics of low RG balls, by virtue of their deep centers of gravity, are biased to shorter skid and longer roll.

Three-piece Construction

A three-piece ball consists of a core, a weight block, and a shell, shown in Figure 7. Core material of three-piece balls is less dense, or lighter per unit volume, than the shell or weight block. A weight block denser than either shell or core is put into a position to add the top weight necessary to compensate for material removed when the grip holes are drilled or to shift for dynamic effect.

Figure 7:   Construction of a Three-piece Ball

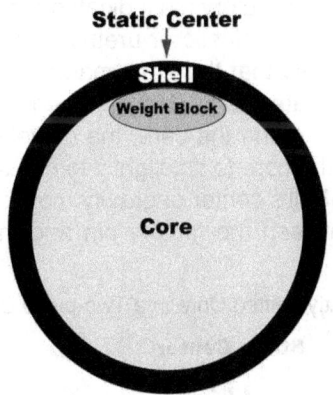

The three-piece category included Columbia's U-Dots, Yellow Dots, and White Dots; Brunswick's Rhinos, AMF's Angle series, and most of Ebonite's balls, including the Thunderbolt D/B. All of these had shallow weight blocks, the center of the top weight being closer to the surface of the ball than to the geometric center. These would be classified as high RG today.

Because the centers of gravity of three-piece single weight block balls are usually closer to the surface of the ball, they tend to offer more resistance to the force of lift, but they typically skid farther and roll later. Therefore, a three-piece ball can benefit a bowler whose normal release type makes his ball skid a shorter distance and roll sooner. An example of a release type that can benefit from a high RG ball is the high roller.

Columbia's Vector II was a three-piece ball, but its deep-set weight block close to the geometric center would place this ball in the low RG category. The Vector II did not act like a standard three-piece ball when it rolled down the lane, and it was highly inappropriate for a bowler with a high track close to the grip holes.

Modern Design Considerations

During the 1980s and 1990s, tipping of the core to one side of the mold during pouring of the shell material presented ball manufactures a marketing problem. Because, the core tipped to varying degrees, the factory pin came to rest in a position that put the static center various distances away from it.

Accidentally Shifted Core

With two-piece balls, the factory pin indicates the center of the weight lobe. The factory pin is a plastic or urethane dowel upon which the core sits in the mold, so that the shell material may flow completely around the core. As late as the 1990s, when the hot shell material flowed into the mold around the core, the dowel bent away from the hotter side, causing the core to tip slightly to one side of the mold. As the core moved, the ball's center of gravity moved with it, causing the distance to grow between the factory pin and the center of gravity. See Figure 8.

Figure 8: Accidently-shifted Core in a Two-piece Ball

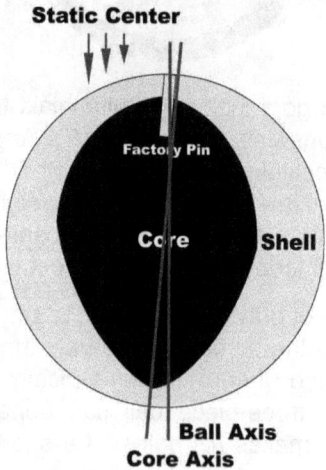

The final, undrilled ball's static center, indicated by the factory punch mark, often migrated several inches from the center of the factory pin (see **Modern Design Considerations**). These were termed **pin out**. **Such a ball has a slight built-in axis gyration that cannot stabilize because the axis of the ball and the core cross each other.** Occasionally, the static center would have to be marked on the other side of the ball from the pin — an extreme situation that presented a marketing dilemma.

Although a few people preferred pin out balls, most preferred the factory pin to be close to the static center; this was termed **pin in**, because the pin was usually inside the label. Many pin out balls were sent overseas to remove them from the American market, but this was not a good long-term solution.

Deliberately Offset Core

Eventually, someone reasoned that the marketing problem could be solved if the core were forced into a position that could dictate where the static center would come to rest, ideally within three or four inches of the pin, The core was then tightly secured in the mold, with its axis offset from that of the ball, before the shell material was poured. See Figure 9.

Figure 9: Deliberately Offset Core in a Two-piece Ball

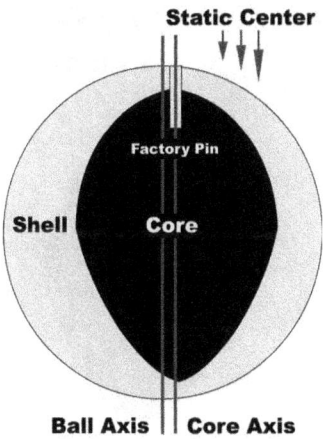

A while later, after some experimentation, it was thought that the offset core, considered a minor nuisance, could be characterized positively. A smaller, secondary pin was inserted in the core to be seen on the surface of the ball. This pin marked the core's center of gravity that was named the **mass bias**. **Such a ball has built-in axis gyration that cannot stabilize because the axis of the ball and the core, although parallel with each other, are never the same.**

Advertising campaigns were launched that included this new concept. The offset core, with its built-in instability, could be used to extend the skid length and, because the ball's center of gravity and the weight masses associated with the factory pin and the mass bias were all fighting for stable positions relative to the ball's axis, the break point was delayed further. When the ball gained enough traction, it began to hook, even when unstable. The skid, roll, hook, reaction was augmented with a secondary hook reaction termed *flip*. The flip created an even steeper angle of attack to the pins. So, what began as an anomaly was turned into a marketing advantage that remains with us to this day.

Asymmetric Core

Today, cores are offered that are not the same shape from side to side to achieve more severe dynamic effects. These are called *asymmetric*, and the odd shapes amplify the reaction characteristics seen in the offset core. See Figure 10.

Figure 10: Asymmetric Core in a Two-piece Ball

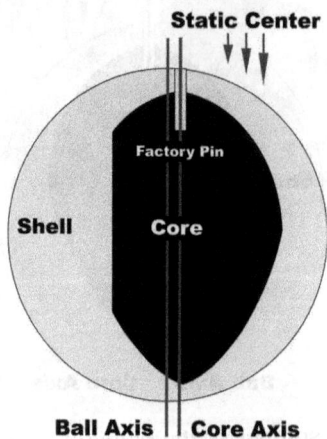

Wherever a dense core has a portion closer to the surface, a weight mass exists, with its own center of gravity. Additional weight masses off of the axis of rotation, including weight blocks added to the core, make the competition for stability around the ball's axis more intense. *What results is a longer skid, a longer period of instability, a hook resulting from traction on the lane surface, and, as the weight centers are trying to reach some kind of agreement with*

the ball's axis, a flip with its steep angle of attack to the pins. Most of these masses never achieve a stable relationship with each other; therefore, the ball's axis is not stable when it hits the pins. Hence, the lane condition must favor the ball to maximize control and pin carry.

> Note: *The objectives of Dynamic Customization cannot be accomplished with a ball having an asymmetric core.* Such a design is used to maximize skid and angle of attack for all release types.

Factors Influencing Ball Choice

Now let's take a look at some factors in the bowling environment that influence the choice of ball for a particular release type.

Ball to Lane Friction

The strongest influence on the hooking capability of a ball is friction. A high-friction lane surface was once called *slow*, while a low-friction lane surface was once called *fast*.

The greater the friction between the ball and the lane, the shorter its skid after touchdown and the earlier the ball hooks. To counter the effects of too much traction, (dry lanes, hooking *back ends*), choose a lower-traction ball to lengthen skid and reduce hook.

The less the friction between the ball and the lane, the longer the ball skids after touchdown and the later the ball hooks, if at all. To counter the effects of too little traction (long oil, heavy oil, extensive carry down), choose a higher-traction ball to shorten skid and increase hook.

Total Ball Weight

A ball need not be heavy to resist deflection. Within reason, it needs only to have its mass concentrated in the proper places. The significance of this assumption is that it is possible to select total ball weight based on how the weight centers are positioned. *Because Dynamic Customization increases the stability of the ball, it is appropriate to drop 1 – 2 pounds in total ball weight to achieve*

better pin carry. Such is especially true with modern, low-resistance pins.

To adjust deflection, take into consideration not only the bowler's ball speed, but which hand the bowler uses to deliver the ball, because the lane surface is different from the left to right halves. ***Choose a lighter-weight ball if more deflection would be beneficial.***

Weight Centers

Ball reaction strongly depends on internal weight centers. A **weight center** is any area in which the density of material is greater than that surrounding it. These involve the relative density of cover and core material, the size and shape of any added weight blocks, and the location of these weight blocks relative to the grip center.

In addition, the distance of an imbalance from the axis can have an effect on the typical dynamic characteristics of a particular ball's design. ***The closer the collective imbalance (including all weight centers) is to the axis of rotation, the more closely the dynamics of a high RG ball resemble those of a ball that is core-dense — a low RG.*** It will tend to skid shorter and roll sooner if another high-magnitude weight center, such as top or bottom weight does not exist.

The farther the collective imbalance (including all weight centers) is from the poles of the axis of rotation, the more closely the dynamics of any ball resemble one that is shell-dense — a high RG. If starting with a high RG ball, it will tend to skid longer and roll later. If another high-magnitude weight center exists, the ball may never stabilize into a roll before hitting the pins.

Note: If starting with a low RG ball for a bowler with a high track close to the grip, do not position the factory pin over three inches from the positive axis pole, lest the track flare over the grip holes. Although such positioning of the factory pin may increase the spherical diameter of the track, the imbalance should pull the grip away from the track, and the flare will be minimal.

Positioning of weight centers is always a compromise, but an educated compromise is better than guesswork. An imbalance can be used to stabilize the roll of the ball before impact and to optimize the angle of attack and the amount of deflection to yield a superior pin-carrying ball. ***The best ball in terms of consistency is one that*** is statically imbalanced on the dodo scale but is dynamically balanced by the time it hits the pins.

Handedness

Because only 9% of the wear occurs on the left side of the lane, a potentially longer skid and a greater angle of attack are in effect for left-handed bowlers. This suggests that the imbalance should initially be closer to the positive axis pole than for a right-hander with the same release type. Depending on the diameter of the bowler's track, a hole may have to be drilled in the positive axis pole to shift the lateral imbalance toward the negative pole, lessening skid, promoting roll, and lessening the angle of attack.

Hand Position

The track on a Dynamically Customized ball should not devolve from dynamic balance into dynamic imbalance before impact if (1) the static center is close to the working weight mass, (2) both have initially been placed close to an axis pole, and (3) there is no other imbalance. The track may flare initially with a normal release and *may flare longer if the bowler changes his hand position at the release.*

The more the thumb side of the hand is pointed down (adduction of the hand), the higher the positive axis pole and the longer the ball skids after release and the later it hooks. The ball will be unstable for a longer distance down the lane, but it should become dynamically balanced before pin impact. *Dynamic Customization yields a ball whose axis stabilizes in the first half of the lane, compensating for variances in roll pattern caused by small inconsistencies in hand position at the release.*

Note: A high track with low ball speed suggests the need for a heavier positive axis pole. A low track with high ball speed suggests the need for a heavier negative axis pole.

---

5 Bowling Ball Dynamics

To **Dynamically Customize** a ball, you need a clear understanding of a ball in rolling motion. Ball reaction, or dynamics, are determined by:
- **Ball speed in translational (linear) motion**
- **Hand position** at the release
- **Force of lift and turn in angular (rotational) motion**
- **Frictional interaction of the ball with the lane.** The greater the friction, the less the ball skids after touchdown on the lane, and the earlier the ball hooks. The less the friction, the more the ball skids after touchdown on the lane, and the later and less the ball hooks, if at all.
- **Strongly influential weight characteristics internal to the ball.** These involve the relative density of cover and core material (low vs. high RG), the size and shape of any weight centers (symmetrical core vs. asymmetric core), and the location of any added weight blocks.

Weight Centers

Weight distribution refers to the amount and location of weight centers (including the ball's center of gravity) in an undrilled or a drilled bowling ball. The mass of a **weight center** is denser than the material surrounding it.

When using the dodo scale, regardless of how many individual weight centers are present inside, a ball will have only one single place (**center of gravity**) where the center of all static weight is located, usually marked on the surface of the ball and designated the **static center**. The ball's center of gravity, whether drilled or undrilled, along with any other internal masses (weight centers that have their own centers of gravity) are collectively called an **imbalance**.

Because of unavoidable inconsistencies in the thickness of the shell during molding, or due to the presence of one or more dense weight centers to a ball, either through the shape of the core or added weight blocks, a ball may have multiple weight centers. In this case, the actual static center may not lie directly over a weight block.

The location of the center of gravity usually shifts as a result of drilling holes, becoming a *resultant static center* when marked on the ball surface. The static center of a plugged, undrilled ball may not be in the same place as it was in the new, undrilled ball. The only conclusion that can be made about a static center without understanding the design of the ball is that the center of gravity lies somewhere between the surface of the ball and the *geometric center*, the physical center of the ball. If a ball is balanced in all directions on the dodo scale, you can assume that the center of gravity is located at the geometric center, and the ball is statically balanced, but not necessarily dynamically balanced.

Note: For a ball to be considered *perfectly balanced*, it must have no static imbalance on the dodo scale and no dynamic imbalance when it is in gyroscopic motion.

Moment of Inertia

The *moment of inertia* of a body is a measure of its resistance to rotating, just as mass is a measure of resistance to translational motion, or moving in a straight line. *A homogeneous ball has a natural moment of inertia that is increased when the center of its mass center is not at the geometric center of the ball.* The increase is equal to the mass multiplied by the square of its distance to the ball's axis of rotation. For example, from **Perceptive Bowling, "Weight Distribution within a Bowling Ball"**, comparing a deep weight center (1.5" from the axis) of two ounces with a shallow one (3" from the axis), The shallow weight center exerts four times the influence (Deep: $2.0 \times (1.5)^2 = 4.5$; Shallow: $2.0 \times (3.0)^2 = 18.0$).

Each weight center has its own *center of mass* and moment of inertia. In combination with shell friction and relative shell and core densities, it is the moment of inertia of one or more weight centers that is responsible for altering a ball's dynamics.

Some useful assumptions can be made about the moment of inertia:

- The farther the weight center from the axis of rotation, or the more massive (not in size; in mass) the larger the moment of inertia. *A large moment of inertia has a greater potential to destabilize the roll of the ball. If the weight center is directly on the axis of rotation, the ball is the most stable.*

- The closer the weight center to the axis of rotation, or the less massive the weight center, the smaller the moment of inertia. *A small moment of inertia can also mean greater stability in the roll of the ball.*

The imbalance of a dynamically-imbalanced ball is not on the axis of rotation. *When a dynamic imbalance is present, the axis of rotation is not motionless. Its poles move in a circle, or gyrate (wobble), exhibiting a flared track on the ball surface.*

The widest pole gyration (greatest wobble and flair) and the least stability occurs when the imbalance is halfway between the positive axis pole and the track, at the leverage point. If a great imbalance exists, the ball may never stabilize into a consistent roll before hitting the pins.

Note: A good visual reference point for the bowler is the gyrating positive pole of the axis of rotation. He cannot see the negative pole as the ball is rolling down the lane.

The least axis gyration occurs when the imbalance is directly on the axis, often called true axis weight or when it is directly under the track (greatest lope). In this case, one may or may not see a flared track.

Gyroscopic Motion

Gyroscopic motion (***body rotation***) is used to provide stability and maintain a fixed orientation of a rotating body. Gyroscopes typically provide direction stability for ships and airplanes.

When a body is spun about an axis, it is, in effect, a gyroscope. A body spinning about an axis will exhibit stability, and it will resist change in the direction of its rotation axis. This resistance is known as the ***gyroscopic effect***. For example, the faster a bicycle wheel (a gyroscope) turns, the greater is the ***gyroscopic inertia***, and thus the more stable is the bicycle and the easier it is for the rider to maintain balance.

Gyroscopic stability is a consequence of Newton's first law (the ***law of inertia***), which states that ***a body in motion (or at rest) tends to remain in the same motion (or at rest) unless the body is acted upon by an external force***. For greatest stability, most of the gyroscope's mass should be as far away from its axis of rotation as possible and symmetrically distributed about the axis — for example, a disc with a large heavy rim. The mass distribution away from the axis of rotation is often characterized by the ***radius of gyration***, which is the square root of the axial moment of inertia divided by the mass of the body.

The ***extension of an object*** (the further the mass from the object's center; a larger radius) turning about its axis slows down its rotation. Likewise, the ***retraction of an object*** (the closer the mass to the object's center; a smaller radius) turning about its axis speeds up its rotation. Although the total mass of the object is unchanged, the distance of the mass from its axis of rotation has changed, altering the speed of rotation, explaining why figure skaters spin faster as they draw their arms in toward their bodies.

A rolling bowling ball is a gyroscope, subject to all of the physical laws imposed on any rotating body. Depending on release type, forward momentum, and force of lift, the ball tends to maintain its rotational speed and axis orientation, countered by friction with the lane surface and altered by the position and masses of imbalances within the ball itself. The extension/retraction phenomenon may be shown in bowling balls wherein rotation accelerates while an imbalance migrates toward an axis pole.

Precession

When a force, such as lift, is imparted to a bowling ball at the release, the ball begins to rotate and touches down, skids, rolls, and forms a track on its surface. The ball rotates around its axis. In response to this rotation, the axis itself rotates, changing its orientation; this action is called *precession*. The axis is said to *precess*.

Torque-free Precession

Counterclockwise rotation of the ball around its axis causes an internal, counterclockwise motion of the axis itself; this movement is called *torque-free precession*, and it tends to keep the positive axis pole turned in a direction back toward the right-handed bowler. It is classified as torque-free because no external force operates on the axis. Because our illustration focuses on the positive axis pole, let's use *positive precession* as a working term.

Positive precession helps to keep the ball from rolling out, maintaining the skid a longer distance. The same is true for a left-handed bowler who imparts a clockwise rotation to the ball; positive precession occurs in a clockwise direction back toward the left-handed bowler.

This type of precession is comparable to that shown by a freely-rotating gyroscope, except that the friction between ball and lane slows the rotation, counters precession, and promotes end-over-end roll of the ball.

Torque-induced Precession

If a mass lies between the geometric center of the ball and an axis pole, it provides an additional external force, or torque, that presses down on the axis. The greater the mass or the closer the mass to an axis pole, the greater the torque. This is an example of *torque-induced precession*. *Torque = Force applied x lever arm*. In this case, the lever arm is the distance between the location of the downward-applied force and the geometric center of the ball along the axis of rotation. Figure 11 shows the influence of the length of the lever arm on the torque caused by identical weight centers.

Figure 11: Influence of the Lever Arm on Torque

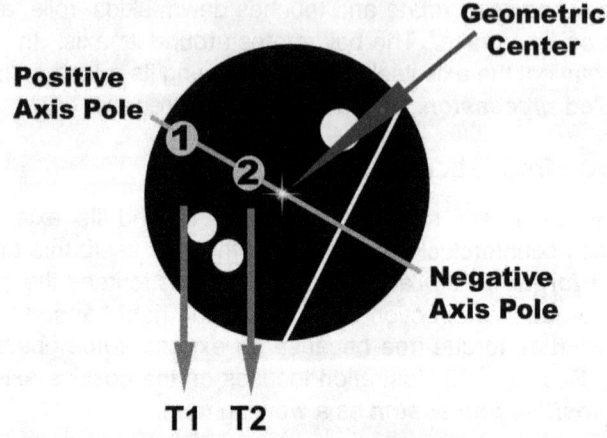

1 = Weight Center 4" from geometric center (4" lever arm)
2 = Weight Center 1" from geometric center (1" lever arm)
   Weight Center 1 = Weight Center 2
   T1 = Torque 1; T2 = Torque 2
   Torque 1 is greater than Torque 2

Depending on the direction of the rotation and the pole upon which the downward force is pressing, the axis pole tends to migrate (precess) toward or away from the bowler. If the mass is near the positive pole, positive precession may be increased; if near the negative pole, positive precession may be reduced. Figure 12 compares torque-free with torque-induced precession.

Figure 12: Torque-free vs. Torque-induced Precession

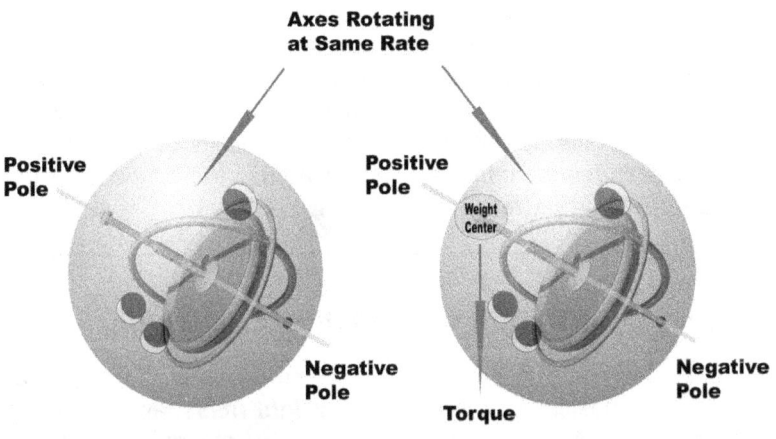

Torque-free Precession   Torque-induced Precession
Positive Axis Poles Rotate Toward Reader

Some useful assumptions can be made about torque-induced precession of the axis of rotation:

- *The closer the imbalance is to an axis pole, the greater the potential for torque-induced precession.* This placement of the imbalance affords less resistance to the application of lift and turn; this is especially true for high RG balls. *Therefore, off-axis placements of imbalances can interfere with the bowler's ability to apply rotation to the ball and limit the number of effective hand positions.*

- A mass on the positive axis pole exerts a downward force on the positive axis pole. In response, the ball tends to turn inward toward the bowler. *A constant downward force on the positive axis pole helps to delay the hook, inducing a sharper angle of attack into the pins and lessening deflection.*

- A mass on the negative axis pole exerts a downward force on the negative pole. In response, the ball tends to turn outward, away from the bowler. *A constant downward force on the negative pole helps to make the ball hook* earlier, inducing a shallower angle of attack into the pins, and allowing more deflection.

Note: When a mass is directly on an axis pole, torque-induced precession can work all of the time, helping to increase or decrease the angle of attack and to minimize or maximize deflection, while not interfering with the stability of the ball's roll. ***Thus, precession can be used to adjust the angle of attack and deflection pattern.***

Positive Axis Weight vs. Negative Axis Weight

If the release-specific procedures recommended in this book are followed, the position of the *working weight mass*, as indicated by the pin, is locked into position. The center of gravity of the ball (excluding the full roller), rests fairly close to the ball's axis, and the positive axis pole is said to be *loaded*. Figure 13 shows a ball in such a starting configuration.

Figure 13:   A Ball with a Loaded Positive Axis.

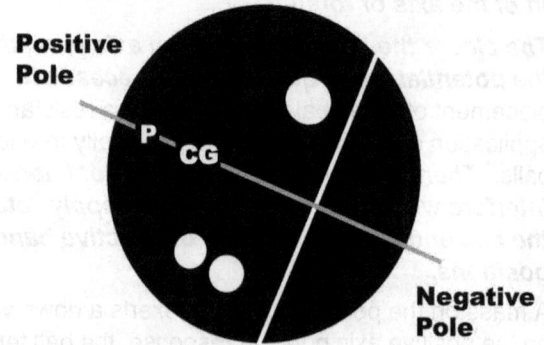

What can one do with a ball with a loaded axis? When the maximum-allowable lateral weight remains close to the (loaded) positive axis pole, this effects a later break point, a steeper angle of attack, and less deflection for a particular ball. Another advantage of loading the axis pole is that the imbalance remains on the positive side of the ball track. Figure 14 shows a comparison of results from placing the imbalance (***Series A***) on the positive axis pole or (***Series B***) above the fingerholes.

Figure 14: Comparing a Loaded Axis Pole with a Loaded Fingerhole Imbalance Location for Five Release Types

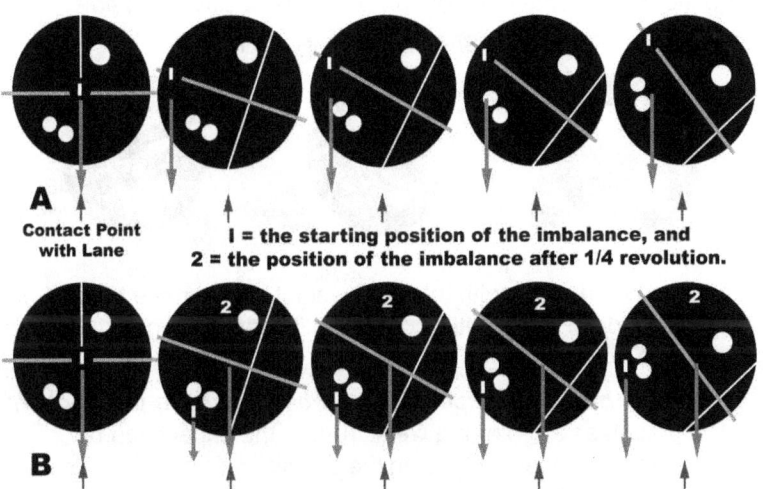

Series A shows the spatial relationship between the location of the downward force (down arrows) of the loaded axis pole imbalance position and the point of contact of the ball with the lane (up arrows). **Note that initial location of the imbalance (number 1) does not change relative to the axis, and the downward force remains constant, which is vital to the application of torque that increases positive precession.** Also, the force always remains on the positive side of the track.

Series B also shows the spatial relationship between the location of the downward force (down arrows) of the loaded fingerhole imbalance position and the point of contact of the ball with the lane (up arrows). **Note that initial location of the imbalance (number 1) changes relative to the axis, as shown by the number 2, and the force does not remain constant, disturbing the application of torque necessary for enhanced positive precession.** Also, at least in the Low Roller and the High and Low Spinner release types, the force moves to the negative side of the track.

The center of gravity can be moved in a direction along the axis by drilling a balance hole in the positive axis pole. The deeper the hole, the closer this weight mass moves toward the center of the ball, until finally, it passes the center and moves on to load the negative axis pole. This position represents an earlier break point, a shallower angle of attack, and more deflection for a particular ball. Figure 15 shows the progressive shift of the center of gravity in response to the depth of a hole drilled in the positive axis pole.

Figure 15: Progressive Shift of Center of Gravity

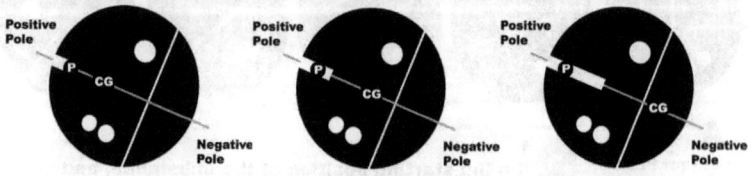

Working in conjunction with total ball weight and surface traction, it is possible to adjust the position of the ball's center of gravity to favor pin carry on pocket hits.

- *If a bowler is experiencing weak leaves in the pocket*, such as a 5-pin or a weak 10-pin, the impact can be strengthened by loading the positive axis pole. In this case, remove only enough lateral weight to make the ball USBC-compliant.

- *If a bowler is experiencing strong leaves in the pocket*, such as a 4-pin or a strong 10-pin, the impact can be weakened by unloading the positive axis pole to the point of loading the negative axis pole. Again, care must be taken not to shift over one ounce to the negative side, because only one extra legalization hole is allowed.

Both of these strategies begin with the layouts recommended in this book, as modified by drilling into the positive axis pole in accordance with careful observation of pin carry over several trials.

Stability vs. Instability

The geometric center of a ball delivered down a lane is in linear (translational) motion, and any imbalance off of the axis of rotation moves in a circular path around the axis. *If the ball has more than one weight center, these centers compete for position on the axis, eventually establishing the most stable orientation possible in the time available. As the centers get closer to the axis, the speed of rotation of the ball increases.* If the center of the imbalance arrives at the axis of rotation, the weight centers are said to be *in agreement* with the ball's angular (rotational) motion, and the axis stops gyrating. At this point, there is no flair, and the ball is rolling stably around its new, resultant axis, the **preferred spin axis**. However, if the weight centers are far apart, their spatial relationship may not allow them to reach agreement, and the ball will not be stable when it hits the pins.

Given that the lane and pin deck are well-maintained, a common cause of inconsistent pin carry is that a ball's imbalance is not on the axis of rotation at impact. When a ball is dynamically imbalanced when it hits the pins, its axis is still gyrating. As the ball rolls toward and through the pins, the imbalance moves up (away from the lane surface), forward (toward the pins), down (toward the lane), and back (away from the pins). The imbalance can be in different, unpredictable positions in its rotation at impact with the pins. *Such instability will never give consistent results from similar pocket hits.*

Effective Mass

What is effective mass? It is the **resistance to force** of an object (determined by experimentation) as modified by an external or internal configuration. A ball thrown at a wall may hit with a given force in a five mile/hour wind, but with a greater force (larger effective mass) in a 40 mile/hour tail wind or with a lesser force (smaller effective mass) in a 40 mile/hour head wind.

The effective mass of a tennis racket increases with the tightness of the player's grip. A golfer wearing cleats on his shoes has a larger effective mass, and his golf ball has a smaller effective mass when rolling through tall grass. Also, if a boxer keeps his back foot in contact with the floor, he essentially increases his effective mass by that of the earth itself, making him able to apply more force.

The effective mass of a dynamically imbalanced bowling ball rolling down the lane does not stay constant. Its effective mass is greatly influenced by the rotation of the ball's internal weight centers around its axis. The position of these weight centers determines the force with which it hits the pins.

Placement of weight centers relative to the grip holes represents a double-edged sword; although it can cause a ball to skid just far enough, roll stably, and hit the pins effectively, it can just as easily

49

make the ball skid too far, roll unstably and hit the pins ineffectively. **Depending on the location of the imbalance relative to the track, a dynamically imbalanced ball may lope and/or wobble.**

Lope

Lope is the alternate speeding up and slowing down of the translational (straight line) motion of the ball rolling toward the pins. Lope results from the imbalance being very close to, or under, the track, tumbling over and over, more or less in line with the path of the ball. There is no wobble of the axis if the imbalance is directly under the track and no other imbalance exists.

Lope cannot be seen well from behind. To detect lope, we should observe from the bowler's swing- or balance side, midway down the lane and from a distance. The greater the magnitude of the imbalance, the more pronounced is the lope. Figure 16 illustrates the action of lope diagrammatically.

Figure 16: Lope in a Rolling Bowling Ball

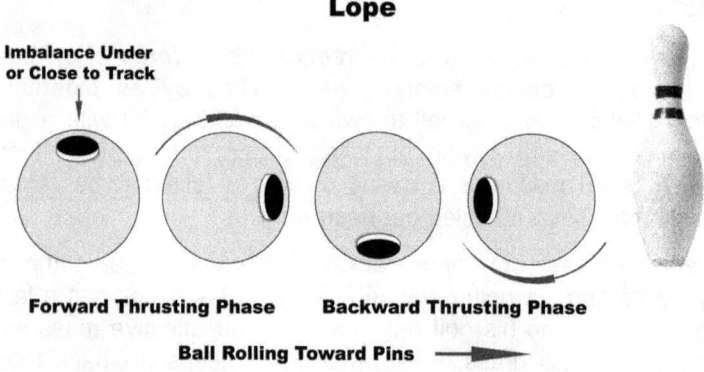

Forward Thrusting Phase: Half of the time, the weight center comes from the midpoint of the back half of the ball, over the top, toward the pins to the midpoint of the front half. When this occurs, the speed of the weight center in motion **adds to the forward speed** of the ball. If the ball contacts the pins when the weight center is moving toward the pins, **the ball's effective mass is greater,** and it will appear to hit the pins harder.

Backward Thrusting Phase: The other half of the time, the weight center comes from the midpoint of the front half of the ball, around the bottom, away from the pins to the midpoint of the back half. When this occurs, the speed of the weight center in motion **subtracts from the forward speed** of the ball. If the ball contacts the pins when the weight center is moving away from the pins, **the ball's effective mass is smaller**, and it will appear to hit the pins more softly.

A loping bowling ball hits with the consistency of a boxer pulling his punch one-half of the time. Another way to think of lope is to imagine a child riding on a tricycle going forward at a constant, slow rate of speed. If the child lunges forward, the tricycle speeds up momentarily; if he lunges backward, the tricycle slows down momentarily.

Wobble

Wobble (gyration of the axis of rotation) results from the presence of an imbalance between the track and an axis pole. **Both poles gyrate, unlike a child's top, wherein one pole is held in place (the point) and the other axis pole is the only one that gyrates.**

Note: **Wobble of both poles is not the result of precession**, because when a ball has no imbalance or if the imbalance is directly on the axis of rotation, no wobble occurs. Precession occurs whenever the ball rotates around its axis.

Wobble is greatest when the imbalance is halfway between the track and the positive axis pole, at the leverage point. When the ball rotates around its axis, **the poles of the axis dip from one side to another** like the wings of a plane, first one side, then the other. But, **they also move forward and backward, varying both the ball's effective mass and its deflection pattern through the pins.** Like the example of lope, the imbalance tumbles over and over toward the pins, but it's position causes the poles to gyrate more widely, causing the visible flair of the track. Figure 17 illustrates the action of wobble diagrammatically.

51

Figure 17: Wobble in a Rolling Bowling Ball

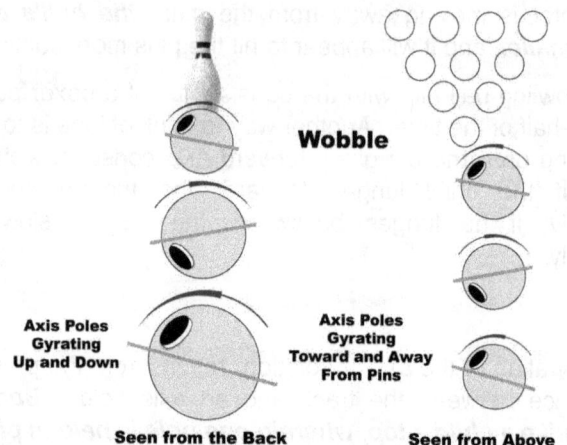

Half of the time, the imbalance will be coming from the midpoint of the back half of the ball, over the top, toward the pins to the midpoint of the front half. The other half of the time, the imbalance comes from the midpoint of the front half of the ball, around the bottom, away from the pins to the midpoint of the back half.

Because the weight center is between the track and an axis pole, the ball not only speeds up and slows down, it turns into the headpin in one phase and away from the headpin in the other. If the ball contacts the pins when the axis is turning toward the headpin, the ball will **deflect less** and appear to hit the pins harder. This can be indicated by strong leaves, such as a right-hander's 4-pin, 9-pin, strong 10-pin, or 4-9 split. If the ball contacts the pins when the axis is turning away from the headpin, the ball will **deflect more** and appear to hit the pins more softly. This can be indicated by weak leaves, such as a right-hander's 5-pin, 8-pin, weak 10-pin, or 8-10 split.

Modern Layouts

Most modern layouts offered by pro shops today involve factory pin placements close to the fingerholes, as shown in Figure 14 B. These layouts position the largest weight mass fairly close to the track. This factory pin placement is often accompanied by a static center placement farther away from the track. Such an arrangement yields a combination of lope and wobble, especially in high RG balls. Presumably, these layouts are suggested to use instability to enhance skid and delay the break point, thereby increasing the angle of attack through the pins.

Naturally, scores have increased over the years, but this spike in scoring is not mainly the result of grip layouts. Rather, the resistance of today's pins is no match for a high-traction reactive resin bowling ball on a blocked synthetic lane surface. **The frequency of off-pocket strikes has increased remarkably, but no one has demonstrated a significant increase in the carrying percentage of solid pocket strikes.**

Problems caused by lope and wobble are not well understood by skilled bowlers and shop professionals; they do not have an appreciation that an imbalance may be in various, unplanned positions when the ball hits the pins. Instability of the axis and inappropriate deflection as the ball rolls through the rack of pins continues to cause unpredictable leaves, resulting in confusion, frustration, and disappointment.

6 Recommendations for Various Release Types

Players of the past have used all release types with success, their eyesight, ability to hit targets, and the suitability of their deliveries to individual lane conditions notwithstanding. *Each release type has its own strong and weak characteristics.* These players overcame the weaknesses of their particular release types with ball speed, strong hand action, and determination beyond the capability of most bowlers.

Goal

The most glaring characteristic of a release type is its ability or lack of ability to carry all of the pins on solid pocket and slightly off-pocket hits. Over the years, I have observed that pin carry on such hits is not the strongest point of the very high- or very low-tracking release types. *If one is to maximize success, pin carry on solid pocket hits must be addressed and optimized, if not for each person, for each release type.*

Therefore, the following recommendations are based on the premise that the track with the highest pocket pin-carrying percentage, is associated with a low roller release type. The *Dynamic Customization* method involves ball selection and layouts that have the effect of decreasing the spherical diameter of a high track and increasing the spherical diameter of a low track, the full roller type being the exception. *When a ball has been Dynamically Customized according to the release-type recommendations with no extra hole, it starts off with the longest skid, the steepest angle of attack, and the least deflection on pocket hits that the layout allows.* An extra hole drilled into the positive axis pole serves

55

to shorten skid, decrease the angle of attack, and increase deflection at the same time.

Note: *A ball with a symmetric core is necessary to successfully accomplish the objectives of Dynamic Customization.*

Organization

The *information under each release type* below is organized as follows:

- Overview
- Selection of an appropriate ball
- Additional preparation of the ball surface
- Suggested layout(s)
- Post-drilling adjustments to the layout

Recommendations in the tables under the heading **Ball Selection** address how a particular release type interacts with the lane in forming a skid, roll, hook pattern to ensure the optimal angle of attack and deflection pattern to match collective pin resistance. Today's pins are considered to be of low resistance; pin resistance (effective mass of a pin) increases with pin weight, elasticity, diameter of the base, and internal weight distribution.

Table 3 is a summary of strategies that use various factors to effect specific changes in ball dynamics. These generalizations may not apply completely to all release types, but they help the reader recall specific recommendations later.

Table 3: Summary of Strategies

Change	Characteristic	Strategies
Shorter Skid / Earlier Roll	Ball surface properties	Select high-traction ball surface and/or roughen it
Longer Skid / Later Roll	Ball surface properties	Select low-traction ball surface and/or polish it

Table 3: Summary of Strategies

Change	Characteristic	Strategies
Decrease Track Diameter	Ball construction	Select high RG
	Placement of imbalance	Load positive axis pole
	Hand position	More turn at release
Increase Track Diameter	Ball construction	Select low RG
	Placement of imbalance	Load negative axis pole
	Hand position	More roll at release
More Hook	Ball construction	Select high-traction ball surface and/or roughen it
	Placement of imbalance	Load positive axis pole
	Hand position	Firm wrist at release
Less Hook	Ball construction	Select low-traction ball surface and/or polish it
	Placement of imbalance	Load negative axis pole
	Hand position	Less wrist extension at release
Earlier Break Point	Ball construction	Select high-traction ball surface and/or roughen it
	Placement of imbalance	Load negative axis pole
	Hand position	Firm wrist at release
Later Break Point	Ball construction	Select low-traction ball surface and/or polish it
	Placement of imbalance	Use axis-leverage type of layout; ensure stability of axis before impact
	Hand position	Less wrist extension at release

Table 3: Summary of Strategies

Change	Characteristic	Strategies
Optimized Deflection Pattern / Pin Carry	Ball construction	Select best total weight to accommodate pin resistance; most subjective, probably between 13.5 and 15 pounds
	Placement of imbalance	Load positive axis pole; after careful trials, drill extra hole in positive axis pole in 1/4-ounce increments

With the exception of the full roller, an imbalance between the leverage point and the positive axis pole gives a more predictable ball reaction on a common lane condition. The *desired starting layout* positions the factory pin approximately one-quarter the way from the positive axis pole toward the track, while the recommended position of the static center is between the grip center and the pin.

Remember that the lower (smaller) the track, the closer the positive axis pole is to the grip center. Finger or thumb weight is added by shifting the grip center up or down on the grip layout centerline. Another way of looking at this layout is that the factory pin is positioned in the positive lateral quadrant of the ball, as determined by the grip layout centerline and the line perpendicular to the track (the *S-P line*).

Note: *It is very important to select a ball with only the amount of top weight needed to compensate for the weight removed by drilling the grip holes.* Too much top weight after drilling may cause prolonged axis gyration, forcing the hole to be drilled in the static center to decrease the skid distance. This measure also may not allow the removal of sufficient lateral weight to be USBC-compliant.

Additional adjustments can be made for fast ball speed, left-handedness, and low-friction lane conditions.

Full Roller

A full roller track extends around the entire circumference of the ball; running through the grip center between the thumbhole and fingerholes. Its spherical diameter is 13.5", or half of the circumference of the ball. The axis of rotation is parallel with the lane surface, and the track is perpendicular to the lane.

Figure 18: Full Roller Release Type

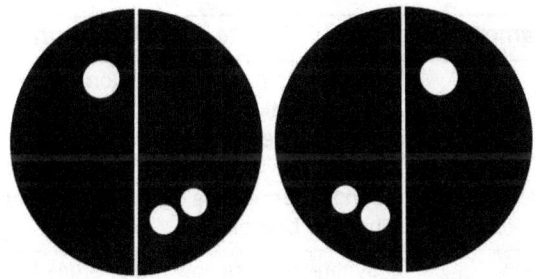

Because there is no axis tilt, the full roller should have the most traction, but it actually has the longest skid distance of the roller-tracking balls, probably because of thumb interference at the release. The absence of axis tilt causes the full roller to impart the least spin to the pins upon impact, resulting in a lower percentage of off-center pocket strikes.

Of all roller types, the full roller has the least potential deflection, the tendency to be pushed off course after impact with a pin. However, due to excessive skid, the full-roller may not phase into a complete roll upon impact.

Table 4: Summary of Full Roller Dynamics

Factor	Unique Characteristics
Track Circumference	Equals the ball circumference
Spherical Diameter	13.5" (half of ball circumference)
Axis Tilt	None; axis of rotation is parallel with lane surface; track perpendicular to lane
Track Position to Grip	Track runs through grip center
Traction Potential	Theoretically the most traction, but longest skid of any roller-tracking ball, especially when an imbalance is present

Ball Selection

The goal is to stabilize the full roller's axis and adjust its deflection pattern, rather than to modify the shape of its ball reaction. Because a full roller tracks inside the grip and skids a great deal, stability of the axis is essential. Therefore, selection of an appropriate ball based on its construction and surface properties is preferred over weight center shifts.

Table 5: Ball Selection Parameters for Full Roller

Parameter	Recommendation
Surface	Medium to maximum traction, depending on lane condition and ball speed; optimize skid after trial deliveries by altering surface. Dulling the finish with fine Scotch Brite or 400 sandpaper may be helpful, especially left-handed bowlers.
Construction	Symmetric core, low RG to promote early roll
Top Weight	Low (2.0 – 3.0 ounces, depending on the size of the hand)
Total Weight	Select 15 pounds maximum for higher ball speed and/or low traction lane condition, select 14 pounds for lower ball speed, high traction lane condition, or low pin resistance.
Deflection Pattern	Optimize deflection pattern with total ball weight, surface traction, and drilling of extra hole after trial deliveries.
Lope / Wobble	A primary objective is to stabilize roll by minimizing lope; remove as much top weight as possible without shifting weight to the bottom of the ball. *Do not use any lateral imbalance; it may result in tracking over the fingerholes or the thumbhole.*

Layout

Two layout summaries for the full roller release type are shown in Figure 19 and Figure 20. In both layouts, the factory pin and static center are 6.75 inches from both axis poles.

Figure 19: Full Roller Layout A

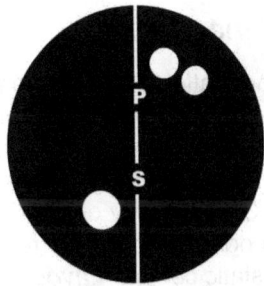

Place the S-P line directly on the ball track, near the center of the grip, with the static center closer to the thumbhole. Factory pin placement closer to the fingerholes may lengthen skid and delay roll; this position may benefit bowlers on higher-traction lane conditions.

Figure 20: Full Roller Layout B

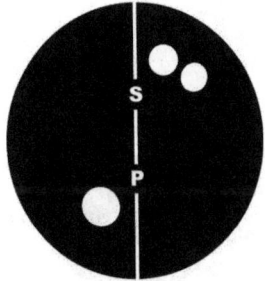

Place the S-P line directly on the ball track, near the center of the grip, with the static center closer to the fingerholes. Factory pin placement closer to the thumbhole may reduce skid and promote earlier roll; this position may benefit bowlers on lower-traction lane conditions.

Post-drilling Adjustments

To *lessen skid while increasing deflection* through the pins, drill a hole in the positive axis pole (optional, depending upon ball speed). Shifting just less than one ounce to the negative axis pole may be especially helpful for left-handed bowlers and for right-handed bowlers on conditions with a strong back end reaction.

Note: Placing the pin/static center close to an axis pole of a full roller could render bottom weight and flare the track over the grip holes. A hole drilled on the bottom of the ball to equalize top and bottom weight could be directly on the ball track.

Importance of Adhering to the S-P Line

It is important to ensure placement of both the static center and the pin on the S-P line when attempting **Dynamic Customization** for non-full roller release types. Compare the balls in Figure 21, which represents three possible layouts for ball with a low-tracking release types. **Layout A** places the static center and 3' pin directly on the S-P line, with the pin 2.5" from the positive axis pole. This is a correct layout for a ball with the pin fairly close to the static center. **Layout B** places the static center directly on the S-P line, but, to avoid shifting lateral weight to the negative side of the grip center, the 4" pin has been placed above the S-P line, but still the same 2.5" from the positive axis pole.

Figure 21: Non-adherence to the S-P Line

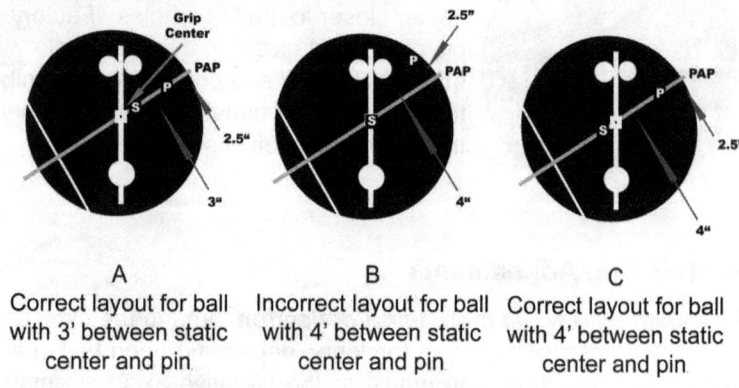

A	B	C
Correct layout for ball with 3' between static center and pin	Incorrect layout for ball with 4' between static center and pin	Correct layout for ball with 4' between static center and pin

Layout B is incorrect because the static center and the pin occupy two different perpendicular relationships to the track. The relationship between these masses makes it more difficult for the ball to stabilize before impact, interrupting its deflection pattern through the rack of pins. **Layout C** is the correct, more stable configuration; the negative lateral weight in the ball is negligible.

High Roller

A high roller has a slightly smaller track than the full roller; its spherical diameter is approximately 12", resulting in a 10-degree tilt of the axis of rotation. The track is approximately 3" from the middle fingerhole.

Figure 22: High Roller Release Type

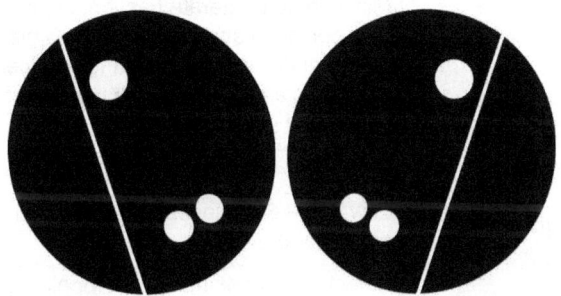

A high roller reaction features the most traction and shortest skid distance of the roller-tracking balls. Because the axis is tilted, the ball imparts more spin to the pins than the full roller. It shows the *least potential deflection of all semi-roller types*.

Table 6: Summary of High Roller Dynamics

Factor	Unique Characteristics
Track Circumference	Slightly smaller than ball circumference
Spherical Diameter	Approximately 12"
Axis Tilt	10 degrees from vertical
Track Position to Grip	Approximately 3" from middle fingerhole and usually closer to the thumbhole
Traction Potential	Most traction, shortest skid of roller tracking balls

Ball Selection

The initial goal is to increase the length of skid, delaying the break point while maintaining stability of the axis.

Table 7: Ball Selection Parameters for High Roller

Parameter	Recommendation
Surface	Minimum to moderate traction, depending on lane condition and ball speed; optimize skid after trial deliveries by altering surface. Shine the ball to a high luster with rubbing compound or 600 wet sandpaper.
Construction	Symmetric core, high RG to lengthen skid
Top Weight	Low (2.0 – 3.0 ounces, depending on the size of the hand)
Total Weight	Select 15 pounds maximum for higher ball speed and/or low traction lane condition; select 14 pounds for lower ball speed, high traction lane condition, or low pin resistance.
Deflection Pattern	Optimize deflection pattern with total ball weight, surface traction, and drilling of extra hole after trial deliveries.
Lope / Wobble	A primary objective is to stabilize roll by minimizing wobble; remove as much top weight as possible without shifting weight to the bottom of the ball.

Layout

The layout summary for the high roller release type is shown in Figure 23.

Figure 23: High Roller Layout

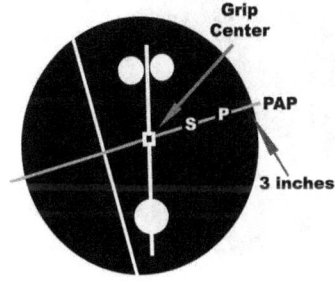

Position the factory pin approximately 3" from the positive axis pole (PAP). Remember that the static center is closer to the grip center. To add finger weight to extend skid and delay roll, move the grip center down on the grip layout centerline by 1/2" – 1".

Note: Should the angle of the S-P line to the grip layout centerline naturally place the factory pin in the positive lower quadrant, consider moving the grip center down to ensure USBC-compliant finger/thumb weight. However, if the track is close to the thumbhole, avoid placement of the factory pin in the positive lower quadrant, otherwise, the track may flair over the thumbhole.

Post-drilling Adjustments

To maintain a longer skid, leave as much positive lateral weight as possible. If the ball is USBC-compliant, do not drill an extra hole. After significant trials, if necessary to *increase deflection*, drill a hole in the positive axis pole (optional, depending upon ball speed), removing 1/4 ounce at a time. *When pin carry is optimal, do not remove any more weight from the positive axis pole.* This modification may be especially helpful for bowlers on stale lane conditions with weak back end reactions. If there is too much top weight after drilling the grip holes, consider drilling a hole in the static center, if it does not cause a problem with gripping the ball. This measure may not remove sufficient lateral weight to make the ball USBC-compliant.

Low Roller

A low roller track is slightly smaller than the high roller's. Its spherical diameter is approximately 10.5", with a 20-degree axis tilt. The track is usually 3" to 5" from the middle fingerhole.

Figure 24: Low Roller Release Type

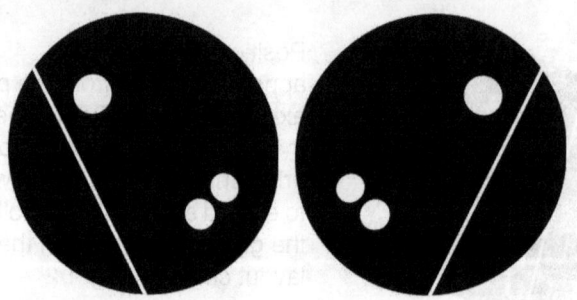

A low roller reaction features less traction and a longer skid distance than the high roller. Greater axis tilt transfers more spin to the pins, resulting in a higher percentage of off-center pocket strikes. *Because the low roller deflects more after impact than the high roller, it takes a wider path through the pins, seemingly carrying the pins most effectively of all release types.*

Table 8: Summary of Low Roller Dynamics

Factor	Unique Characteristics
Track Circumference	Slightly smaller than high roller
Spherical Diameter	Approximately 10.5"
Axis Tilt	20 degrees from vertical
Track Position to Grip	Approximately 3" from middle fingerhole and usually closer to the thumbhole
Traction Potential	Less traction; longer skid than high roller

Ball Selection

The goal for this release type is to support an already-superior ball dynamic. The low roller has a longer skid than the high roller, with optimum attack angle, deflection, and pin carry on solid and off-center pocket hits. As far back as the late 1960's, I observed the superior pocket pin carry of this release type with its lower track. Then, as now with the USBC, the ABC allowed a maximum post-drilling difference of three ounces from top to bottom of the ball, along with a maximum of one ounce difference from front to back and from side to side.

In an effort to keep the lateral and front-to-back weight ABC-compliant, drillers usually centered the grip over the label, which itself was centered over the static center, or punch mark. Bowlers with the low-track release types had a distinct pocket pin-carrying advantage because the ball's axis was angled so that the positive axis pole was almost touching the palm of the hand. Their balls could carry almost three ounces of positive axis weight. Bowlers with higher (larger diameter) tracks could not take advantage of the loaded axis, lest the lateral weight in their balls exceed one ounce. *The straight-up, over-the-label drilling layout was never fair to all bowlers.*

Note: One may ask, "*If the low roller is the ideal release type, why do you recommend loading the positive axis pole on this or any other ball with a small diameter track?*" The answer to this question is that, **no matter how small the spherical diameter of the track, with its inherent long skid, the layout must begin with the axis stabilized.** Stability requires that the factory pin and/or static center be locked into a position close to the positive axis pole before subsequent adjustments are made to angle of attack and deflection by drilling an extra hole.

Table 9: Ball Selection Parameters for Low Roller

Parameter	Recommendation
Surface	Moderate traction, depending on lane condition and ball speed; optimize skid, if necessary, after trial deliveries by altering surface. Dulling the finish with fine Scotch Brite or 400 sandpaper may be helpful, especially left-handed bowlers. The higher the traction, the larger the spherical diameter of the track.
Construction	Symmetric core, **high RG to maintain size of track** (low RG would tend to raise track unnecessarily)
Top Weight	Low (2.0 – 3.0 ounces, depending on the size of the hand).
Total Weight	Select 15 pounds maximum for higher ball speed and/or low traction lane condition; select 14 pounds for lower ball speed, high traction lane condition, or low pin resistance.
Deflection Pattern	Optimize deflection pattern with total ball weight, surface traction, and drilling of extra hole after trial deliveries.
Lope / Wobble	A primary objective is to stabilize roll by minimizing wobble; remove as much top weight as possible without shifting weight to the bottom of the ball.

Layout

The layout summary for the low roller release type is shown in Figure 25.

Figure 25: Low Roller Layout

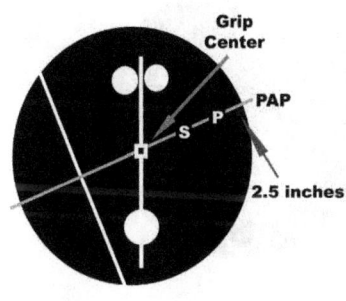

Position the factory pin approximately 2.5" from the positive axis pole (PAP). Remember that the static center is closer to the grip center. Do not add finger or thumb weight by moving the grip center up or down. If the pin is over 4 inches from the static center, the static center may rest on the track side of the grip layout centerline. This is acceptable.

Note: Should the angle of the S-P line to the grip layout centerline naturally place the factory pin in the positive lower quadrant, consider moving the grip center down to ensure USBC-compliant finger/thumb weight.

Post-drilling Adjustments

Because the objective with this release type is to **maintain skid length without altering track diameter**, some lateral weight may need to be removed to preserve the original track diameter; this is somewhat dependent on ball surface properties, but can be accomplished by drilling an extra hole in the positive axis pole. **If pin carry is optimal, do not drill any extra hole, unless the lateral weight is not USBC-compliant.** Only after significant trials, drill the hole, removing 1/4 ounce at a time. If there is too much top weight after drilling the grip holes, consider drilling a hole in the static center, if it does not cause a problem with gripping the ball.

High Spinner

The high spinner has a track smaller than the low roller, with a spherical diameter of approximately 9" and a 30-degree axis tilt. The track is approximately 5" to 7" from the middle fingerhole.

Figure 26: High Spinner Release Type

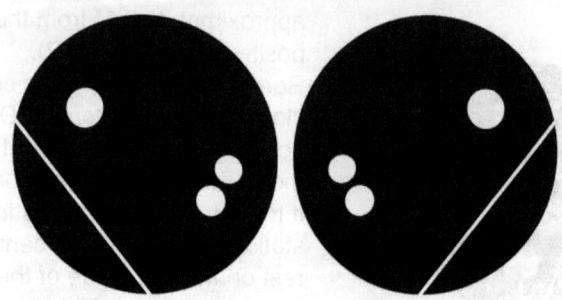

A high spinner reaction features less traction and a longer skid distance than the low roller. More axis tilt means more spin transfer to the pins, but the percentage of off-center pocket strikes may not be high because of deflection after impact with the headpin.

Table 10: Summary of High Spinner Dynamics

Factor	Unique Characteristics
Track Circumference	Slightly smaller than low roller
Spherical Diameter	Approximately 9"
Axis Tilt	30 degrees from vertical
Track Position to Grip	Approximately 5" to 7" from middle fingerhole and usually closer to the thumbhole
Traction Potential	Less traction; longer skid than low roller

Ball Selection

The goal is to lessen the skid, enlarge (raise) the track, and decrease deflection. The high spinner has an even longer skid and greater deflection than the low roller.

Table 11: Ball Selection Parameters for High Spinner

Parameter	Recommendation
Surface	Moderate to maximum traction, depending on lane condition and ball speed; optimize skid, if necessary, after trial deliveries by altering surface. Dulling the finish with fine Scotch Brite or 400 sandpaper may be helpful, especially left-handed bowlers.
Construction	Low RG to lessen skid and promote earlier roll
Top Weight	Low (2.0 – 3.0 ounces, depending on the size of the hand)
Total Weight	Select 15 pounds maximum for higher ball speed and/or low traction lane condition; select 14 pounds for lower ball speed, high traction lane condition, or low pin resistance.
Deflection Pattern	Optimize deflection pattern with total ball weight and surface traction. If ball exhibits strong leaves, drill extra hole, shifting axis weight to negative pole after trial deliveries. Otherwise, leave lateral weight neutral or positive.
Lope / Wobble	Stabilize roll by minimizing wobble; ensure that all top weight is removed by drilling the grip holes.oles.

Layout

The layout summary for the high spinner release type is shown in Figure 27.

Figure 27: High Spinner Layout

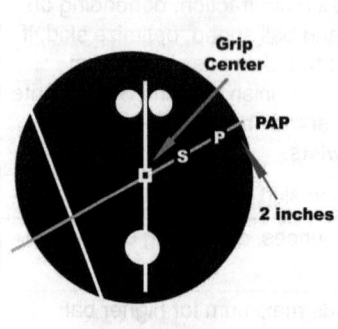

Position the factory pin approximately 2" from the positive axis pole (PAP). Remember that the static center is closer to the grip center. Add optional thumb weight by moving the grip center up on the GLC by no more than 1/4". Because the track is low, the factory pin being in the positive lower quadrant will probably not cause a problem and may actually promote earlier roll. If the pin is over 3 1/2" inches from the static center, the static center may rest on the track side of the grip layout centerline. This is acceptable.

Post-drilling Adjustments

Because the objective with this release type is to *lessen skid length*, remove all positive lateral weight by drilling an extra hole in the positive axis pole. Only after significant trials, drill the hole, removing 1/4 ounce at a time, creating negative axis weight, if necessary. *When pin carry is optimal, do not drill out any more weight.*

Low Spinner

A low spinner has an even smaller track than that of the high spinner. Its spherical diameter is approximately 7.5", giving it about a 40-degree axis tilt. The track is more than 7" from the middle fingerhole.

Figure 28: Low Spinner Release Type

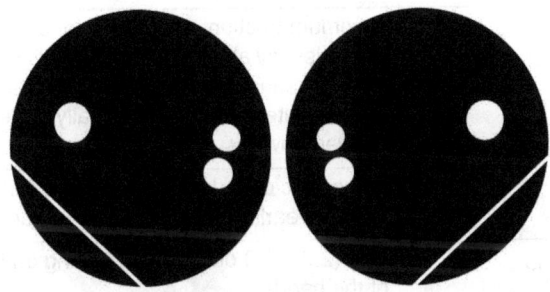

A low spinner reaction features the least traction and longest skid distance of all release types. Although it imparts the most spin to the pins, the low spinner ball deflects the most after impact. Consequently, this ball shows the lowest carrying percentage of solid pocket and slightly light hits; although carry of extremely light or slightly heavy pocket hits may be the best of all types.

Table 12: Summary of Low Spinner Dynamics

Factor	Unique Characteristics
Track Circumference	Slightly smaller than high spinner
Spherical Diameter	Approximately 7.5"
Axis Tilt	40 degrees from vertical
Track Position to Grip	More than 7" from middle fingerhole and usually closer to the thumbhole
Traction Potential	Least traction; longest skid of all dynamic types

Ball Selection

The goal is to decrease the length of skid and raise the track, while decreasing deflection.

Table 13: Ball Selection Parameters for Low Spinner

Parameter	Recommendation
Surface	Maximum traction; optimize skid, after trial deliveries, by altering surface. Dulling the finish with 320 sandpaper and medium-coarseness Scotch Brite is helpful, especially for left-handed bowlers.
Construction	Symmetric core, low RG to lessen skid, promote earlier roll, and raise the track
Top Weight	Low (2.0 – 3.0 ounces, depending on the size of the hand)
Total Weight	Select 15 pounds maximum for higher ball speed and/or low traction lane condition; select 14 pounds for lower ball speed, high traction lane condition, or low pin resistance.
Deflection Pattern	Optimize deflection pattern with total ball weight and surface traction. If ball exhibits weak leaves, drill extra hole, shifting axis weight to negative pole after trial deliveries. Otherwise, leave lateral weight neutral or positive.
Lope / Wobble	Stabilize roll by minimizing wobble; ensure that all top weight is removed by drilling the grip holes.

Layout

The layout summary for the low spinner release type is shown in Figure 29.

Figure 29: Low Spinner Layout

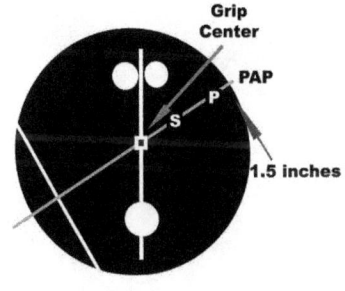

Position the factory pin approximately 1.5" from the positive axis pole (PAP). Remember that the static center is closer to the grip center. Add optional thumb weight by moving the grip center up on the GLC by 1/2" to 1". Because the track is so low, placement of the factory pin in the positive lower quadrant will probably not cause a problem and may actually promote earlier roll. If the pin is over 3 inches from the static center, the static center may rest on the track side of the grip layout centerline. This is acceptable.

Post-drilling Adjustments

Because the objective with this release type is to *lessen skid length*, all positive lateral weight should be removed by drilling an extra hole in the positive axis pole until negative axis weight is created. Only after significant trials, drill the hole, removing 1/4 ounce at a time. **When pin carry is optimal, do not drill out any more weight.**

75

7 Layout and Adjustment

The following is a sequence to be used when physically positioning the factory pin and static center in a symmetric-core ball relative to the grip holes. Apply these *Dynamic Customization* techniques in conjunction with the release-specific information given in *Recommendations for Various Release Types*.

No grip fitting or drilling instructions are described below. However, steps for on-lane observation are included, as is a brief procedure for the three-piece ball, as wall as some thoughts on the location of an extra hole and tips for observing pocket pin carry.

Procedure for a Two-piece Ball

The two-piece ball is the most common design on the market today. The basic symmetric-core design is shown in Figure 30. There are many variations on this design (asymmetric core) that are not discussed in this book.

Figure 30: Basic Two-piece Ball Design with a Symmetric Core

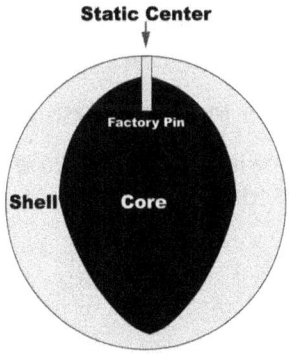

77

Follow these instructions in order and think through each preparation, layout, and post-drilling step carefully, always keeping in mind the spatial relationships among the track, the grip center, the factory pin, and the positive axis pole.

Preparation of the New Ball Before Drilling

Always take the time to prepare the ball properly prior to drilling. Follow these steps in order.

1. Weigh the ball to verify static center position and top weight magnitude. Indicate a new static center with the letter *S*, if necessary.

2. Determlne the spacial orientation of the long axis of the core passing through the pin.

    To do this, draw a line, the S-P line, from the static center (S) to the middle of the factory pin (P).

    Figure 31: Drawing the S-P Line on a New, Undrilled Ball

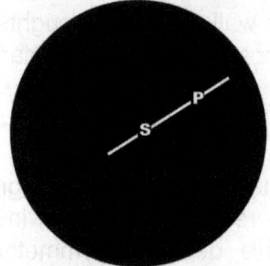

3. Extend the S-P line 4" to 5" on either end. You will use this longer line later to help you place the factory pin in different locations relative to the ball track and the grip layout centerline (GLC).

Finding the Track on a Previously-drilled Ball

Using another of the bowler's *properly-fitted* balls to determine the location of the ball track, do the following:

1. Trace the track with a wax pencil.

Figure 32: Tracing the Track

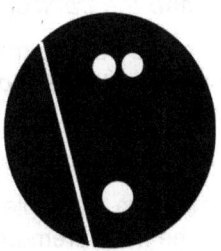

Note: Use only a properly-fitted ball to trace the track. A poorly-fitted ball interferes with a bowler's release, making it impossible to determine the preferred release from the position and angle of the track.

2. Draw the grip layout centerline (GLC) and mark the grip center.

Figure 33: Drawing the Grip Layout Centerline

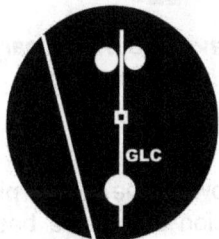

3. Draw a line perpendicular to the track (S-P line), running through the grip center.

Figure 34: Drawing the S-P Line on a Previously-drilled Ball

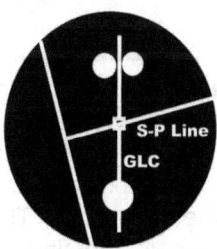

4. Extend this line all the way around the ball to meet the track on the opposite side (bottom) of the ball.

5. Measure the length of the S-P line from track to track and divide the result by two to get the **distance between the positive axis pole and the track** on the S-P line.

6. Subtract the length of the track-to-track S-P line from 27; this gives the **spherical diameter (SD) of the track** used later to classify release type.

7. Mark the positive axis pole with the wax pencil.

8. With a protractor, measure the angle of the S-P line to the GLC. Write this on the measurement sheet.

Figure 35: Angle Between S-P Line and Grip Layout Centerline

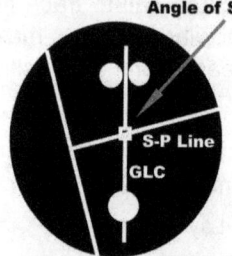

At this point, you have the necessary information to begin Dynamically Customizing the new ball.

Laying Out the New Ball

The major decision is how far the factory pin should be from the axis of rotation. Your decision should be based on the release type, designated by the size and location of the ball track. See the recommendations in the chapter titled **Recommendations for Various Release Types**. These take into account the bowler's ball speed, the bowler's handedness, and the most common lane conditions encountered.

Note: The angle of the track and its distance from the grip holes are important. Unless the bowler's track is at least two inches from the thumbhole, avoid placement of the factory pin (or static center in a three-piece ball) in the positive lower quadrant, as this may move the track over the thumbhole. The same reasoning applies to a track that is close to the fingerholes; the positive upper quadrant may be problematic.

1. Before marking the new ball, decide where the static center and factory pin should lie on the S-P line, relative to the track and the positive axis pole.

   Refer to the information in Recommendations for Various Release Types. The recommended spatial relationship of the elements is: Track – Grip Center – Static Center (S) – Factory Pin (P) – Positive Axis Pole, as shown in Figure 36.

Figure 36: Arrangement of Elements on a Two-piece Ball

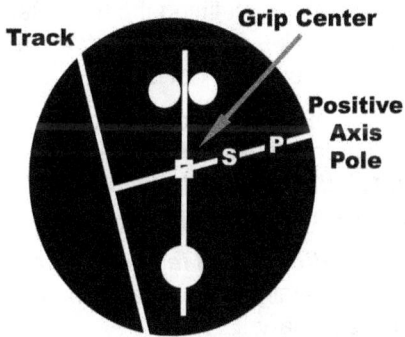

2. Mark the new ball, transposing the S-P line from the previously-drilled ball. **Position both the static center and the factory pin on the S-P line the recommended distance from the positive axis pole.** Placing the static center between the grip center and the factory pin ensures that drilling the grip holes removes as much of the imbalance at that point as possible.

3. After the correct distance is established between the factory pin and the positive axis pole, measure down the S-P line from the positive axis pole to find and mark the grip center.

4. Draw a grip layout centerline through this point at the correct angle, ensuring that the S-P line on the new ball remains perpendicular to the track. Unless the ball track is parallel with the grip layout centerline, expect some finger or thumb weight to result.

5. *To add finger weight*, simply shift the grip downward along the GLC. *To add thumb weight*, shift the grip upward along the GLC.

For example, ***strokers*** (with high ball tracks) can benefit from positive lateral weight and finger weight, while ***crankers*** (with low ball tracks) can benefit from negative lateral weight and thumb weight.

Note: If the track is closer to the fingerholes than to the thumbhole, thumb weight is a good alternative, acting like finger weight for a track closer to the thumbhole.

---

6. Drill and completely finish fitting the ball. Remember that ***drilling the grip holes causes the static center to migrate***; the weight block itself does not move.

7. Weigh the drilled ball on the static dodo scale for compliance with USBC tolerances and to locate the resultant static center. ***Find and mark the resultant static center with a small piece of visible adhesive tape.***

   In most competition, a ball is allowed only one extra hole. If the ball is too laterally imbalanced to be USBC-compliant, an extra hole is necessary.

Post-Drilling Adjustments

An extra hole may be necessary to (1) bring the ball within USBC tolerances and/or (2) modify its dynamics. Placement of a ***balance hole*** or ***legalization hole*** should be decided carefully, but a ball can be made USBC-compliant without watching its reaction on the lane.

Even though some adjustment to the location of an imbalance may be necessary, ***it should not be made at the expense of stability of roll at impact. When drilling a hole to modify dynamics, on-lane observations are necessary, and these may take a considerable amount of time.*** One must be careful to preserve the desired dynamic effect that the layout was chosen to achieve. See ***Thoughts About the Location of an Extra Hole*** at the end of this chapter.

When it is necessary to drill an *extra hole*, follow a logical series of steps:

1. *After several practice deliveries, making sure that the grip is completely comfortable, begin observing the ball's dynamics. See Tips for Observing Pin Carry, below.*
2. *Mark with visible adhesive tape the following additional locations*:
   - The *positive axis pole*, as located on a previous ball before drilling the new ball being tested.
   - The resultant positive axis pole, referred to as the *preferred spin axis (pole)*.
3. Drill a hole in the positive axis pole (not the preferred spin axis pole) to ensure USBC-compliance. Remove only enough material to reduce lateral weight to a fraction less than one ounce. *Remove only 1/4 ounce at a time*
4. Observe more closely as the bowler rolls a sufficient number of deliveries to make sensible conclusions about pin carry on pocket hits. This step takes time and attention.
   - *If observations are inconclusive, do not remove any more material.* Resume on-lane observations when more time is available.
   - *If observations are conclusive and pocket hits result in strong leaves,* drill more deeply into the positive axis pole, *removing only 1/4 ounce at a time* and reweighing the ball.

   It is better to use a small diameter bit and drill the hole deeply, leaving mass remaining close to the surface than to drill a large diameter hole shallower. This method may not be sufficient if there is a large amount of weight in the starting hole location.
5. *Return to the lanes and thoroughly evaluate pin carry on pocket hits.*
6. When pin carry on pocket hits is optimal, do not drill out any more material. *If the ball is not to be used in competition that does not allow plugged balls, the material can be added back via partial plugging.*

Alternative Method: For balls that will not be used in competition that prohibits the use of plugged balls, you may prepare some 1/4-ounce weight disks of the same diameter as the hole; these can be molded from plug. *While observing pin carry, add one at a time to the extra hole, secure them with a styrofoam retainer of an appropriate length, and cover the opening with tape.* It may take more than four of these disks to provide one ounce of lateral weight. Continue observing, adding or removing disks as necessary to optimize pocket pin carry. When the optimum is reached, weigh the ball on the dodo scale for lateral weight, remove the disks, and measure them for thickness. Then pour the same volume of plug into the hole and allow it to set.

Procedure for a Three-piece Ball

The three-piece ball is less common than it was several years ago. However, companies still offer this design, as shown in Figure 37.

Figure 37: Basic Three-piece Ball Design

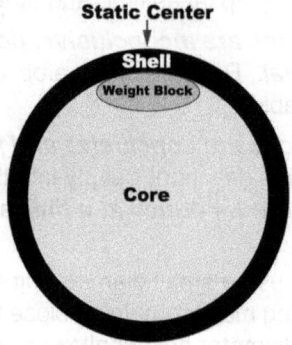

Procedures for a three-piece ball are basically the same as for the two-piece ball with a symmetric core, except that the single weight block is directly under the static center in the undrilled ball. Select a ball surface in accordance with the typical lane dressing pattern with 2.0 – 2.5 ounces of top weight.

There is no S-P line — only an S — to mark the static center. Just like the two-piece ball, the three-piece layout requires a line to be drawn perpendicular to the track at the proper angle to the grip layout centerline, through the grip center to the positive axis pole. *The recommended spatial relationship of the elements is: Track –*

Grip Center – Static Center (S) – Positive Axis Pole, as shown in Figure 38.

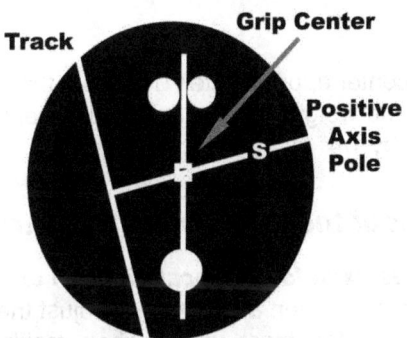

Figure 38: Arrangement of Elements on a Three-piece Ball

Then, it is possible to position the static center at the desired location along this line between the grip center and the positive axis pole.

Brief release-specific recommendations for three-piece balls are as follows.

Full Roller

Place the static center directly on the ball track, near the center of the grip. To adjust the position, move the static center up or down the track, closer to either the fingerholes or the thumbhole.

High Roller

Place the static center approximately 3" from the positive axis pole. Add finger weight by moving the grip center down on the grip layout centerline by 1/4" to 1/2".

Low Roller

Place the static center approximately 2.5" from the positive axis pole. Add finger weight by moving the grip center down on the grip layout centerline by no more than 1/4".

High Spinner

Place the static center approximately 2" from the positive axis pole. Add optional thumb weight by moving the grip center up on the grip layout centerline by no more than 1/4".

Low Spinner

Place the static center approximately 1.5" from the positive axis pole. Add optional thumb weight by moving the grip center up on the grip layout centerline by 1/4" to 1/2".

Thoughts About the Location of an Extra Hole

Four possibilities exist for the location of an extra hole. The first two are most common when attempting to adjust the dynamics of the ball. The are also the most useful when making a ball USBC-compliant. The next two are of doubtful value and may actually ruin an otherwise effective ball.

Into an Axis Pole

When effecting **Dynamic Customization**, drilling into the positive axis pole is the safest method to make the ball USBC-compliant and preserve the dynamic effect. However, it requires selection of low top weight in the undrilled ball.

If the undrilled ball carried a low top weight, the resultant static center should have moved after drilling to a point closer to the positive axis pole. The small imbalance at this point should not be of significant magnitude to exceed top or lateral imbalance limits.

If the undrilled ball carried a high top weight, drilling into the positive axis pole may not be effective. Excessive residual imbalance at the resultant static center may interfere with the desired dynamic effect.

Note: Drilling into the negative axis pole should be done only to shift weight toward the positive pole, and then only if the imbalance is close to the axis. This tactic should not be necessary if the recommendations for release type are followed.

Into the Resultant Static Center

In high top weight balls, this method may be the only way to bring the ball into USBC tolerance. When effecting **Dynamic Customization** with two-piece balls, drilling the extra hole into the resultant static center may be a good way to enhance the desired dynamic effect, if the static center is not close to the factory pin.

Removing most or all of the imbalance at this location allows the weight center at the factory pin to migrate to the axis without competition. At least, removing all imbalance to less than one ounce at this location assures that the ball is within USBC tolerances in all directions.

Into the Pin

Because the factory pin indicates the location of the weight center that will do the desired dynamic work, drilling a legalization hole (or a grip hole) into the factory pin serves no useful purpose and is not recommended. There is always the possibility that an undrilled ball with a high top weight may be drilled for a person with a small hand. Therefore, more than three ounces (USBC maximum limit) of top weight could remain in the drilled ball. If the selected layout did not offset the factory pin very far from the grip center, the resultant static center may coincide with the pin! In this case, the only remedy is to drill into the factory pin / resultant static center location. Drilling into the factory pin removes approximately 1.25 times as much weight as is indicated on standard weight removal charts.

Anywhere Else

This is a haphazard method that should be avoided. If there is not a valid reason to drill an extra hole in a specific location, drill into an axis pole. It is not practical to drill a hole that interferes with gripping the ball or that lies on the ball track.

Note: *When a hole is drilled in a ball somewhere other than in a weight center, uncompensated weight is removed on one side, effectively creating a new, resultant weight center on the opposite side with its own moment of inertia.*

Tips for Observing Pin Carry

Observing pin carry for the purpose of adjusting the position of the ball's center of gravity is different from watching a bowler to adjust the fit of the ball. The purpose of the session is not to instruct on form, unless the bowler is having difficulty acclimating to a new grip.

Note: If a ball has been **Dynamically Customized** according to the release-type recommendations with no extra hole, it starts off with the longest skid and steepest angle of attack that the layout allows.

Test Lane Condition

The bowler should test on a condition that a league or tournament player could expect to encounter after an initial period of carrydown — one to three games. There should not be a great difference between the oiled and dry areas of the lane. If this is not practical, a freshly-dressed condition is usable; just try to wait for the dressing to set in or carry down somewhat before beginning observations.

Settling Down

Because a new ball with a completely clean surface enhances pin carry, *observation should be delayed for a couple of games*, not only to ensure good grip security and a clean release, but to allow the ball to develop a buildup of dressing. Again, do not instruct on form. Wipe the ball off with a dry towel before each observed delivery.

Note: If the bowler is having difficulty with a new grip and/or if the lane condition is unusually slick or dry, one may have to delay the observation session until the bowler is more comfortable with the ball and the lane condition is more useful for testing.

The bowler should be aligned properly for strikes and hitting the pocket regularly before beginning observations. The bowler should try to perform as well as possible in trying to make strikes; no spares should be attempted.

Keeping Track

To be systematic about observations, use a score sheet to make notes. Using the abbreviations described in Table 14 as shown in Figure 39, **record only square or slightly off-pocket hits, sweeping off whatever is left after the first ball of the frame.** It may take two or three games to fill in a one-game scoresheet with pocket hits.

Table 14: Abbreviations for Observation Notes

Small Square	Large Square	
	Right-handed	Left-handed
X	S (Solid), L (Light), H (Heavy), T4 (Tripped 4-pin), M10 (Messenger 10-pin), W5 (Weak 5-pin)	S (Solid), L (Light), H (Heavy), T6 (Tripped 6-pin), M7 (Messenger 7-pin), W5 (Weak 5-pin)
9	S (Strong) or W (Weak) + 4, 5, 7, 8, 9, 10 (Pin number)	S (Strong) or W (Weak) + 4, 5, 7, 8, 9, 10 (Pin number)
8	4-9 (Strong leave), 4-5, 5-7, 5-8, 5-10 (Weak leave)	6-8 (Strong leave), 5-6, 5-7, 5-9, 5-10 (Weak leave)
7	4-5-7, 5-8-10 (Weak leave)	5-6-10, 5-7-9 (Weak leave)

Interpretation

Let's consider each of the three example games shown in Figure 39.

Figure 39: Score Sheet for Recording Observation Notes

Name	1	2	3	4	5	6	7	8	9	10	Total
Brian	9 / S4	8 / 49	X / T4	7 / 457	X / S	X / S	9 / W10	7 / 457	X / W5	X X 8 / S810	
Brian	X / T4	9 / W10	X / S	9 / S10	X / S	X / S	9 / S10	X / S	X / T4	X 8 / 49	
Brian	X / S	X / M10	X / T4	9 / S10	X / S	9 / 4	9 / S10	X / S	9 X 9 / 4	/ S W8	

Game 1: Brian, a right-handed bowler, starts off with a high pocket hit, followed with a strong pocket split and a tripped 4-pin. At this point, one would think that his ball is hooking too early, but it would be wise to observe further. Continuing, he leaves a weak split in frame 4. After solid hits in frames 5 and 6, he leaves a weak 10-pin and a weak split in frames 7 and 8. Barely knocking over the 5-pin in frame

9, he finishes with a solid hit and a weak pocket split in the tenth frame.

Brian is obviously having some trouble with weak hits, but these may be caused by a too-acute angle to the pocket, with the ball finishing behind the headpin. He should be left alone to work out these problems; he may possibly try a different hand position.

Game 2: Brian starts off with a high pocket hit, followed with a weak one. Then, he has seven pocket hits, broken up by two strong 10-pin leaves. He finishes with a solid hit and a weak 8-10 split. **Basically, he has adjusted somewhat to be able to raise his pocket carrying percentage.** At this point, Brian seems to have developed a more effective angle of attack. Again, no action is needed.

Game 3: Brian starts off with a solid pocket hit, followed with a strong light hit and seven solid pocket strikes or strong leaves, before leaving a weak 8-pin on his eleventh shot.

Brian has scored 32 pocket hits that struck 17 times; his pocket pin-carrying percentage is 53%.

Action

What could be done to raise this figure? The percentage of weak, non-carrying hits is 19%, and the percentage of strong, non-carrying hits is 28%. Also, he may be acclimating to the ball and bowling with a bit more confidence.

Judging from his progress during the three games, *it can be concluded that the ball is actually a bit stronger than it needs to be*, suggesting that a slight amount of weight could be removed from the positive axis pole to promote earlier roll, lessening the angle of attack.

What Brian might expect from this measure is a better pin-carrying percentage on the hits that result in strong leaves, while the hits that result in strikes would sustain. The carrying percentage of hits that result in weak leaves may improve because Brian may be able to use a more direct angle to the pocket.

Glossary

Angle of Attack – the angle at which the ball makes its impact anywhere into the rack of pins. A **steep**, or **acute**, angle is more perpendicular to the swingside edge of the lane than is a **shallow** angle. This definition is more general than entry angle, which implies directedness of the ball into the strike pocket.

Axial – situated on an axis.

Axis of Rotation (AR) – an imaginary line perpendicular to the plane of the ball track; equidistant from all points on the track and passing through the geometric center of the ball. The axis has a positive axis pole at one end, oriented toward the center of the lane, and a negative pole at the other end, oriented toward the bowler's swingside channel.

Axis of Weight Core – an imaginary line drawn from the center of the factory pin, through the geometric center of the ball, to the bottom of the core.

Axis Weight – the closeness of the center of gravity of the ball to the ball's axis.

Balance Side – the side opposite the bowling arm; the side of the balance arm.

Body – in physics, an object that has three dimensions, mass, and is distinguishable from surrounding objects

Center of Gravity (CG) – the point at which the entire weight of a body may be considered as concentrated so that if supported at this point the body would remain in equilibrium in any position.

Center of Mass – see Center of Gravity.

Core Dense – see Low RG.

Deflection – a deviation from the direction being followed; in the case of bowling, it is a change in the direction of the ball resulting from an off-center impact with a pin.

Deflection Path – the direction taken by a ball through the rack of pins after impact with the headpin. The greater the deflection, the wider the path; the less the deflection, the narrower the path.

Density – the degree of compactness of a material; the formal definition is mass per unit volume. A quart of feathers is less dense than a quart of lead shot.

Dynamics – the forces and motions that characterize a system:; in the case of bowling, it is the behavior of a ball in translational and gyroscopic motion.

Dynamically Balanced – where the weight centers in a rolling ball are balanced in all directions (radially) around its axis of rotation. There is no gyration of the axis.

Effective Mass – a complex, but well-accepted concept; the resistance to motion of an object (determined by experimentation) as modified by an external or internal configuration.

Extension of an Object – increasing the radial distance of the mass of a rotating object from its axis of rotation.

Flare of the Track – a spreading or **fanning out** of the oil track on the ball as a result of both poles of the ball's rotational axis gyrating in a circle; the axis acts like the wings of an airplane dipping to one side then to the other.

Geometric Center – the exact physical midpoint of the ball.

Head – roughly the first 20 feet of the lane past the foul line.

High RG – the radial distance of a ball's theoretical center of mass is relatively farther from the axis.

High Track – a ball track with a large spherical diameter.

Homogeneous – uniform composition throughout an object.

Imbalance (noun) – the collective mass of all weight centers within the ball. Even though each weight center has its own center of gravity, the imbalance has its own, as well. The center of gravity of the imbalance may or may not coincide with the ball's center of gravity.

Imbalanced (adjective) – a lack of stability, the ball's internal weight centers, or masses, are not in symmetry around the ball's axis of rotation.

Inside – the direction away from the swingside channel.

Layout – the position of the grip holes relative to the location of internal weight centers.

Lever Arm – in the case of a weight center close to a pole of a ball's axis of rotation, the lever arm is the distance between the downward applied force from the geometric center of the ball along the axis of rotation.

Loaded Axis – placement of an imbalance in a position sufficiently close to an axis pole so that all of its associated weight centers can reach agreement soon after entering the rolling phase. The imbalance does not have to be directly on an axis pole, but it must contribute to stabilizing the axis so that it does not gyrate.

Loading – placement of an imbalance in a particular location. The location is said to be loaded.

Low RG – the radial distance of a ball's theoretical center of mass is relatively closer to the axis.

Low Track – a ball track with a small spherical diameter.

Lower the Track – decrease the spherical diameter of the ball track.

Moment of Inertia – a measure of a body's resistance to rotating, just as mass is a measure of resistance to translational motion, or moving in a straight line.

Negative Axis Pole – see Axis of Rotation (AR)

Object – a material thing that can be seen and touched. See Body.

Outside – the direction toward the swingside channel.

Perfectly Balanced – the condition where a ball has no static imbalance on the dodo scale and exhibits no dynamic imbalance when it is in rotational motion.

Pin Carry – number of pins knocked down by the first ball of a frame.

Positive Axis Pole – see Axis of Rotation (AR).

Positive Precession – a working term unique to this book; clockwise (counterclockwise) precession resulting from clockwise (counterclockwise) rotation of the axis.

Post-drilling Adjustment – steps carried out after the grip holes have been drilled and fitted comfortably to the bowler's hand.

Precession – a comparatively slow rotation of the axis of rotation of a spinning body about another line intersecting the axis.

Radial – diverging uniformly from a central point or axis.

Radius of Gyration (RG) – a geometric measure of the moment of inertia. The RG squared, multiplied by the mass is equal to the moment of inertia. The higher the RG, the greater the radial distance of the mass from the axis.

Raise the Track – increase the spherical diameter of the ball track.

Release Type – the interplay of hand position, forward swing speed, angle of the ball to the lane surface, and the force of rotation when releasing the ball, as indicated by the diameter of the ball track and its position relative to the grip holes.

Retraction of an Object – decreasing the radial distance of the mass of a rotating object from its axis of rotation.

Roll – the phase of dynamics when a ball gains enough traction to discontinue skidding.

Shell Dense – see High RG.

Skid – the phase of dynamics before the ball gains enough traction to roll; usually confined to the head area of the lane and beyond, depending on ball speed.

Spherical Diameter (SD) – the distance measured in an arc over the center of the smaller portion of the ball enclosed by the track.

Static Center (SC) – a location on the surface of the ball directly In line with the geometric center of the ball and the ball's center of gravity. The Static Center is often indicated by a punch mark in the shell.

Statically Balanced – a ball is symmetrical in weight from one side to the other when measured on a static (dodo) scale. This is true for comparisons of top/bottom, finger/thumb, and right/left lateral weight.

Swingside – the side of the bowling arm.

Tilt (Axis Tilt) – the axis of rotation is not parallel with the lane; the positive pole is usually further away from the lane than the negative pole.

Torque – a force applied at a given distance from a pivot point. Torque = Force applied x lever arm. In the case of a rolling bowling ball, the axis of rotation may be supplied a downward force by a weight center positioned a given distance (lever arm) from the geometric center (pivot point) of the ball along the axis itself.

Track (Ball) – a ring of lane dressing or a circular pattern of scratches on the surface of a bowling ball that indicate points of contact with the lane.

Wobble – to rotate with an uneven or rocking motion or unsteadily from side to side. In bowling, it is a gyration of the axis of rotation, resulting from the presence of a weight center between the track and an axis pole. This action has been mistakenly referred to as precession, but it is distinct from true precession, because when a ball has no imbalance or if the imbalance is directly on the axis of rotation, no such wobble occurs. Also known as ***teeter***.

Index

A

angle of attack
  adjustment 20
  asymmetric core 35
  ball construction 29
  increasing 53
  left-handed bowler 37
  lessening 37, 48, 90
  optimizing 36, 56
  precession 45
  steeper with flip 34
  steepest 55, 88
  too acute 16
asymmetric core 34, 35
axis of rotation
  angle vs. hand position 23
  close imbalance 36
  competition for stability 48
  defined 21
  deflection 20
  distance from factory pin ... 80
  distance from weight center ... 41
  far imbalance 36
  gyration 51
  loaded 46
  no tilt of full roller 59
  parallel with lane surface ... 59
  stabilizing 21
  tilt of high roller 63
  tilt of high spinner 70
  tilt of low roller 66
  tilt of low spinner 73
  tilt vs. smaller track 26
  torque-free precession 43
  torque-induced precession 43
  track diameter 20
  track flare 22
  wobble 51

B

back ends 35
balance 24
balance hole 82
ball
  choice factors 35
  construction 29
  design 29
  geometric center 40
  speed 39
ball reaction
  determiners 39
  dynamics 15, 39
  predictable 58
  shape 60
  weight centers 36
being on the side 23
blocked lane 16, 18
body rotation 42
bowling pin
  effective mass 56
  elasticity 16
  resistance 36, 53, 56

C

center of gravity 9, 39
  adjusting position 88
  ball 9, 32, 34, 39
  close to axis 46
  competing for stability 34
  core 32, 33
  defined 39
  depth 40
  distance to factory pin 32
  placing along axis 47

progressive shift illustration 48
shifts in drilling 40
weight mass 34
center of mass 40
core
   accidentally shifted 32
   asymmetric 34, 35
   deliberately offset 33
core-dense 20
cover-dense 20
crankers 82

D

deflection
   adjusting 36
   decreasing 36, 71
   defined 16
   increasing 65
   optimal 15
   pin carry 17
   resisting 35
   weight center 20
Dynamic Customization
   ball track 55
   ball weight 35
   benefits 10
   defined 15
   drilling extra hole 86
   fits release type 10
   instructions 77
   no asymmetric core 35
   pocket pin carry 17
   sequence of procedures 26
   stabilized axis 17
   uses symmetric core 56
dynamics
   adjusting break point 20
   adjusting with extra hole ... 82, 86
   ball reaction 15, 39
   defined 16
   full roller 59
   high RG ball 36
   high roller 63

high spinner 70
influence of weight center .. 21
low RG ball 30
low roller 66
low spinner 73
moment of inertia 30, 40
observing 83
strategies of change 56

E

effective mass 53
   bowling pin 56
   concept 49
   rolling bowling ball 49
extension of an object 42
extra hole 83

F

factory pin
   above fingerholes 9
   at static center 29
   close to fingerholes 16
   competing for stability 34
   distance from axis 80
   in positive quadrant 65, 72, 80
   in S-P line 78
   location of extra hole 87
   locked into position 67
   near grip center 87
   placement for full roller ... 61
   placement for high roller ... 65
   placement for high spinner 72
   placement for low roller ... 69
   placement for low spinner .. 75
   two-piece ball 32
fast lane 35
flared track 41
flip 34
friction
   ball to lane 10, 16, 29
   fast lane 35
   influence on hook 35, 39
   skid distance 35, 39

slow lane 35

G

geometric center 40
goals
  ball manufacturers 17
  Dynamic Customization 17
grip center 19
  factory pin 81
  finger/thumb weight ... 58, 65, 69
  full roller track 59
  marking 79, 81
  reference point for scale 19
  relative to static center 85
  relative to track 58
  relative to weight block 36
  S-P line 79
  spatial relationship 78, 85
  static center 81, 84, 85
gyroscopic effect 42
gyroscopic inertia 42

H

heavy oil 35
high RG 20, 30, 31
high track 25

I

imbalance 16, 39
imbalanced 16

L

lane condition
  blocked 18
  favors pin carry 35
  observing pin carry 88
  predictable ball reaction 58
  release type 55
  scoring potential 16
  stale 65
  suitable for testing 88

law of inertia 42
legalization hole 82
leverage point 41, 51
lift and turn 39
loaded axis
  defined 46
  negative pole 48
  positive pole 46
long oil 35
low RG 20, 31
low track 25

M

mass
  ball 21
  collective of weight centers 16
  competing for stability 34
mass bias 33
  competing for stability 34
  origin 33
moment of inertia 40
  assumptions from 41
  defined 40
  individual weight center 87
  large 41
  small 41

N

negative axis pole
  ball speed 37
  drilling into 86
  left-handed bowler 61
  loaded 30, 48
  orientation 21
  precession 45
  strong back end reaction ... 61

O

over-the-label drilling 67

P

path through pins 20
perfectly balanced 40
pin carry
   adjusting with extra hole 65
   alternative observation 84
   ball track diameter 20
   ball weight 36
   cause of inconsistent 49
   clean ball surface 88
   effective track diameter 55
   favored by lane condition .. 35
   goal 17, 55
   low roller release type 67
   observing 48, 83
   optimizing 17
   position of center of gravity 48
   tips for observing 88
pin in 33
pin out 32, 33
positive axis pole 21
   gyration 41
   orientation 21
positive precession 43
precession 43
   influence on skid 43
   positive (working term) 43
   torque-free 43
   torque-induced 43
preferred spin axis 49, 83

R

radius of gyration 20, 42
reactive resin 16
release type
   classifying 25
   determining 80
   elements 18, 23
   five basic 15, 19
   full roller 59
   generalizations 56
   high roller 63
   high spinner 70

ideal 67
low roller 66, 69
low spinner 73
maximizing pin carry 17
modern layouts 16
using information 26
resistance 56
resultant static center 40
retraction of an object 42

S

shape
   ball reaction 17, 60
   core 34, 40
   weight block 36
   weight center 39
shell-dense 20
skid
   asymmetric core 34
   ball construction 29
   blocked lane condition 18
   factory layouts 10, 53
   full roller 59
   generation through wobble 22
   hand position 37
   high RG ball 36
   high roller 63
   high spinner 70
   hole in static center 58
   insight from release type 19
   lane friction 35, 39
   left-handed bowler 37
   lengthening 10, 34, 65, 69
   longest 55, 88
   low roller 66
   low spinner 73
   manipulation 17
   maximizing 30
   positive lateral weight 65
   precession 43
   shortening 30, 37
   three-piece ball 31
   two-piece ball 30
slow lane 35

S-P line 62
   positive lateral quadrant 58
   relative to grip center 79
spherical diameter 25
static center
   at factory pin 29
   in undrilled ball 19
   over center of gravity 39
statically balanced 40
staying behind 23
straight-up drilling 67
strokers 20, 82

T

Taylor, Bill 9, 19, 24
three-piece ball 31
torque-free precession 43
torque-induced precession ...43
true axis weight 41
two-piece ball 29

W

weight center
   adjusting track diameter 20
   ball dynamics 29
   competing for stability 34
   defined 36
   deflection 20
   destabilizing axis 21
   distance from axis 21
   high RG ball 30
   in agreement 49
   low RG ball 30
   positioning 35, 36
   relative density 39
   two-piece ball 9, 29
   working 37
weight disks 84
weight distribution 39
weight mass
   in modern layout 52
   working 46

wobble of axis 51
working weight center 37
working weight mass 46

Figures

Figure 1: Five Basic Release Types 15

Figure 2: The Ball's Axis of Rotation 21

Figure 3: Flare of the Track 22

Figure 4: Swing Plane Hand Position vs. Axis Angle 23

Figure 5: Spherical Diameter of a Track on a Ball 26

Figure 6: Construction of a Two-piece Ball 30

Figure 7: Construction of a Three-piece Ball 31

Figure 8: Accidently-shifted Core in a Two-piece Ball 32

Figure 9: Deliberately Offset Core in a Two-piece Ball 33

Figure 10: Asymmetric Core in a Two-piece Ball 34

Figure 11: Influence of the Lever Arm on Torque 44

Figure 12: Torque-free vs. Torque-induced Precession 45

Figure 13: A Ball with a Loaded Positive Axis. 46

Figure 14: Comparing a Loaded Axis Pole with a Loaded Fingerhole Imbalance Location for Five Release Types 47

Figure 15: Progressive Shift of Center of Gravity 48

Figure 16: Lope in a Rolling Bowling Ball 50

Figure 17: Wobble in a Rolling Bowling Ball 52

Figure 18: Full Roller Release Type 59

Figure 19: Full Roller Layout A 61

Figure 20: Full Roller Layout B 61

Figure 21: Non-adherence to the S-P Line 62

Figure 22: High Roller Release Type 63

Figure 23: High Roller Layout 65

Figure 24: Low Roller Release Type 66

Figure 25: Low Roller Layout 69

Figure 26: High Spinner Release Type 70

Figure 27: High Spinner Layout 72

Figure 28: Low Spinner Release Type 73

Figure 29: Low Spinner Layout 75

Figure 30: Basic Two-piece Ball Design with a Symmetric Core.... 77

Figure 31: Drawing the S-P Line on a New, Undrilled Ball 78

Figure 32: Tracing the Track 79

Figure 33: Drawing the Grip Layout Centerline 79

Figure 34: Drawing the S-P Line on a Previously-drilled Ball 79

Figure 35: Angle Between S-P Line and Grip Layout Centerline .. 80

Figure 36: Arrangement of Elements on a Two-piece Ball 81

Figure 37: Basic Three-piece Ball Design 84

Figure 38: Arrangement of Elements on a Three-piece Ball 85

Figure 39: Score Sheet for Recording Observation Notes 89

Tables

Table 1: Differences Between Goals 17

Table 2: Release Types and Causative Actions 24

Table 3: Summary of Strategies 56

Table 4: Summary of Full Roller Dynamics 59

Table 5: Ball Selection Parameters for Full Roller 60

Table 6: Summary of High Roller Dynamics 63

Table 7: Ball Selection Parameters for High Roller 64

Table 8: Summary of Low Roller Dynamics 66

Table 9: Ball Selection Parameters for Low Roller 68

Table 10: Summary of High Spinner Dynamics 70

Table 11: Ball Selection Parameters for High Spinner 71

Table 12: Summary of Low Spinner Dynamics 73

Table 13: Ball Selection Parameters for Low Spinner 74

Table 14: Abbreviations for Observation Notes 89

www.ingramcontent.com/pod-product-compliance
Lightning Source LLC
Chambersburg PA
CBHW050654160426
43194CB00010B/1932